The Grammar of Kansai Vernacular Japanese

Kevin Heffernan

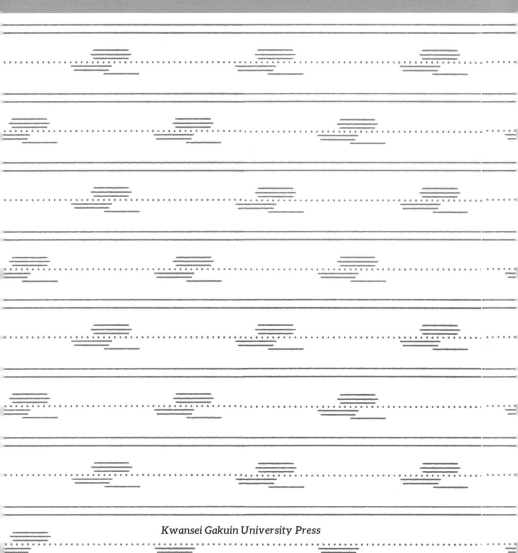

Kwansei Gakuin University Press

Preface

This book was written for intermediate and advanced students of Japanese as a second language, who are living in the Kansai region. Beginner level students who do not yet have a solid understanding of basic Japanese patterns such as しなければならない may find the contents too much. In order to help students of different levels focus on the material of an appropriate level, each vocabulary item, grammatical pattern, and sound pattern presented has been rated for frequency. This rating is based on how often the expression is used, and has a three-point scale: *low*, *medium*, and *high*. High frequency expressions, such as the copula 〜や, are used by everyone all of the time. Low frequency expressions tend to be used rarely or even considered obsolete. Lower level students should only focus on the frequent expressions. Here is the list of the frequency symbols:

Frequency	Symbol
Low	●○○
Medium	●●○
High	●●●

Besides the frequency symbols, the following abbreviations are used throughout the book:

    SJ: Standard Japanese
    VJ: Vernacular Kansai Japanese
    NP: nominal phrase (nouns and な-adjectives)
    VP: verbal phrase (verbs and い-adjectives)
    ます-form: the verb stem form inflected for the 〜ます suffix
          examples: 行きます, 食べます
    ない-form: the verb stem form inflected for the 〜ない suffix
          examples: 行かない, 食べない
    て-form: the verb stem form inflected for the 〜て and 〜

	た suffixes
	examples: 行って, 食べて
plain form:	the uninflected, non-past verb form
	examples: 行く, 食べる
え-form:	the Group I verb stem form that indicates 'be able to,' and ends in an え vowel
	examples: 行ける, 会える
volitional form:	the verb forms exemplified by 行こう, 食べよう, and しよう
Group I verb:	verbs for which the negative is formed by adding 〜aない to the stem
	examples: 行く, 会う, 話す
Group II verb:	verbs for which the negative is formed by adding 〜ない to the stem
	examples: 食べる, 見る
Irregular verb:	the verbs are する and 来る

Almost all of the example sentences in this book are based on actual examples taken from the *Corpus of Kansai Vernacular Japanese.* This corpus is a collection of over 150 hours of recordings of Japanese people native to the Kansai area chatting with each other. Several of the explanations in this book refer directly to the corpus.

    An English translation is provided for each example sentence. The English translations are quite direct, and often literal. Consequently, they may at times feel unnatural. However, this is intentional: A direct, literal translation helps the reader understand the Japanese by matching the Japanese words to their English translations.

Contents

Preface 3

1 The Nature of Vernacular Language 9
    1-1 What is vernacular language? 9
    1-2 Stylistic variation 13
    1-3 Accommodation 16

2 The Structure of Vernacular Language 19
    2-1 The pressure to speak quickly 19
    2-2 Chaining 20
    2-3 Knowing a few words equals much understanding 22
    2-4 Morpheme bundles 25

3 The Copula 29
    3-1 The basic pattern 〜や 29
    3-2 Past tense 〜やった 29
    3-3 Conjunction 〜やって 29
    3-4 Negative copula forms 30
    3-5 Negative past tense copula forms 31
    3-6 Polite SJ usage within vernacular language 32

4 More Copula Expressions 39
    4-1 〜んや and its variants 39
    4-2 そうや and its variants 40
    4-3 Other expressions with や 41
    4-4 Asking questions 42
    4-5 やんか and other expressions of confirmation 44
    4-6 A youthful variant 〜っす 48

5 Basic Verb Forms ... 51
  5-1 Present continuous tense forms ... 51
  5-2 Past tense forms ... 55
  5-3 Command forms ... 57
  5-4 The potential form: ら -dropping ... 58
  5-5 The causative form ... 59

6 The Verbal Negative Suffixes ... 61
  6-1 The basic pattern: Group I and Group II verbs ... 62
  6-2 Lengthening of Group II verbs ... 65
  6-3 Irregular verbs ... 65
  6-4 The past tense ... 67
  6-5 The conditionals ～と, ～たら ... 68
  6-6 The conjunctive forms ～んくて, ～へんくて ... 69
  6-7 Potential negative ... 70
  6-8 Vowel harmony ... 72

7 More Verbal Patterns ... 75
  7-1 Positive obligation: ～なあかん ... 75
  7-2 Negative obligation: ～たらあかん ... 76
  7-3 Permission and advice: ～てええ, ～んでええ ... 77
  7-4 Forms based on ～て＋おく ... 78
  7-5 Request forms ～といて, ～んといて ... 81
  7-6 ～よる ... 83
  7-7 ～はる ... 84

8 Sentence-Final Particles ... 89
  8-1 Overall patterns ... 89
  8-2 な ... 91
  8-3 ねん ... 93
  8-4 で ... 94
  8-5 わ ... 96
  8-6 や ... 96

8-7 っけ ……………………………………………… 99
8-8 さ ………………………………………………… 99

9 って ……………………………………………………103
9-1 Background ……………………………………… 103
9-2 As a vernacular variant of と ………………… 103
9-3 Report the contents of a request, decision, etc. ……… 104
9-4 Repeat what was said …………………………… 105
9-5 Indicate the topic ……………………………… 106
9-6 Clarify something ……………………………… 106
9-7 Emphasize that you already said something ……… 107
9-8 だって …………………………………………… 108
9-9 ってゆうか ……………………………………… 109

10 Expressions of Vagueness ………………………113
10-1 Background …………………………………… 113
10-2 みたいな ……………………………………… 113
10-3 感じ …………………………………………… 115
10-4 なんか ………………………………………… 116
10-5 〜的 …………………………………………… 121
10-6 〜ら, 〜らへん ………………………………… 123

11 The Special Status of 「ん」 ……………………127
11-1 Sentence-final particle ん …………………… 127
11-2 NP ん NP ……………………………………… 128
11-3 こん, そん, あん, どん ………………………… 129
11-4 Nominalizer ん ………………………………… 131
11-5 こんなん, そんなん, あんなん, どんなん ……… 132
11-6 もん …………………………………………… 134
11-7 Verbs ending in る before a nasal sound ……… 135
11-8 ない-form +んない ……………………………… 138

12 Abbreviation, Reduction and Omission······139
12-1 Commonly occurring abbreviations ·············· 139
12-2 [s] sound reduces to an [h] sound ················· 141
12-3 Conjunctions ·· 142
12-4 Case marker omission ···································· 143
12-5 Copula omission ·· 146
12-6 Shortening of long vowels ······························ 147
12-7 Abbreviations of proper nouns ····················· 150

13 Patterns Seen in Adjectives and Verbs········153
13-1 Consonant doubling ·· 153
13-2 Clipping ·· 155
13-3 Vowel coalescence ··· 156
13-4 k-dropping ·· 158
13-5 Small つ changes to う ································ 163
13-6 Reduced forms of the verb しまう ············· 165
13-7 Reduced forms of the verb もらう ············· 168
13-8 Reduced forms of ～て+いく ······················· 170
13-9 ～て+や/あ～ Combine to Form ～た～ ········ 171

1 The Nature of Vernacular Language

1-1 What is vernacular language?

This book is about Vernacular Japanese (which is abbreviated to VJ). Vernacular language refers to the language used in daily conversations with friends and family members. It is the language used with your lover and with your pet dog.

The opposite of VJ is Standard Japanese (which is abbreviated to SJ). SJ refers to the language used by people such as newscasters and salespeople. It is the language used with strangers and in formal settings such as business meetings. It is also the language learned in Japanese language class.

How does VJ differ from SJ? This question can be difficult to answer, as even native speakers cannot easily explain it. The reason is that our decisions about vernacular language—the language you use when chatting away with friends—takes place at the subconscious level. Compare talking to friends to writing an essay. When you write an essay, you think about word choice, sentence voice and paragraph organization. When you write an essay, you consciously choose your language. In contrast, who thinks about such things when talking to friends? You just say what needs to be said, and it all works out in the end. When talking with friends, you unconsciously choose your language. Because vernacular language is used without conscious effort, it is not so easy to understand fully what it is.

Vernacular language has several important characteristics. Let us begin with an example from English: the future tense marker *be going to*. Here is a list of the full range of variation for a single sentence using the future tense marker *be going to*. At the top is the standard, written form. As you move down the list, the form becomes more and more vernacular.

◇　I am going to go now.
◇　I'm going to go now.
◇　I'm goin' to go now.
◇　I'm gonna go now.
◇　I'ma go now.

　　Looking at this list, you can see that the more vernacular sentences are shorter. This is the first important characteristic of vernacular language: It is shorter than standard language.
Now look at the list again, but this time focus on the words that stay the same from one line to the next. There are three of them: *I*, *go*, and *now*. In fact, these three words contain the entire meaning of the sentence, and although it is not grammatically correct, the sentence *I go now* has the same meaning as the sentences in the list. Even though the example sentences vary from standard to vernacular, the meaning does not change. In other words, all of the changes that take place are in the grammatical parts of the sentence. This is the second important characteristic of vernacular language: Almost all of the differences between SJ and VJ take place in the grammatical parts of the sentence.
　　Now let us look at a Japanese example. Do not worry if you do not understand the more vernacular sentences. The purpose of this book is to teach such expressions.

◇　早く行かなければなりません。
◇　早く行かなければならない。
◇　早く行かなあかん。
◇　早お行かなあかん。
◇　早行かなあかん。

　　Again, you see the same two characteristics. The first characteristic is that the more vernacular sentences are shorter. The second characteristic is that all of the changes take place in the grammatical parts of the sentence.

Throughout the rest of this book, the parts of the sentence that change are referred to as variants. Variants are different ways of saying the same thing. For example, 行かなければならない and 行かなあかん are two variants with the meaning 'I must go.'

The lack of a "correct" model

Another important difference between VJ and SJ is the concept of correctness. When you make a mistake on your Japanese homework, the teacher corrects it, and hopefully you try to understand why you made the mistake. Underlying all of this is the assumption that there is a correct way of speaking Japanese. Of course, you can also make grammar mistakes in VJ, but the concept is slightly different. The correct way of speaking SJ is very clear to all native speakers. Most Japanese people learned it as a child. Every primary school student in Japan does 音読 homework almost every day. This involves reading aloud SJ from a textbook. In this way, they learn standard pronunciation and grammar. They do this homework almost daily for about five years as a child, and this reinforces the SJ model. The Japanese word for this model is 規範. VJ is different. Because Japanese children learn VJ from listening to and talking with other people around them, everyone speaks slightly differently, and as mentioned, there are many variants for the same phrase. For example, consider the list of variants for the Japanese word 気持ち悪い 'disgusting':

◇ きもちわるい
◇ きもちわる
◇ きもい
◇ きもっ

Which of these are correct? They all are. However, many Japanese people would never use the expressions きもわるい and きもわる themselves and they might feel that these Japanese expressions are simply wrong. If you ask such a person if you can say

きもわるい or きもわる, or if you ask that person if these expressions are correct, then he or she will most likely say no. VJ does not have a correct model, so it is difficult to decide which is correct and which is not. Keep this in mind when you ask your Japanese friends if such-and-such an expression is correct.

Generally speaking, the farther a vernacular form deviates away from the standard form, the more vernacular it feels. Consider again the list of vernacular forms for きもちわるい. The form きもい, which is near the bottom of the list, is much further away from the standard form than きもわるい. Therefore, relatively speaking, きもい is more vernacular than きもわるい. Similarly, it is more "wrong" so to speak.

The model for spoken SJ is written Japanese. It is recorded in newspapers, novels, and 音読(おんどく) textbooks. Because of that, it is resistant to change. SJ is changing over time, but very slowly. In contrast, VJ does not have a standard model and it is not written down. Nothing is stopping new variants from spreading, and VJ changes quickly. This rapid change leads to notable differences between the older and the younger generations. This is another important characteristic of VJ: Younger and older people speak differently. The language that is introduced in this book is for the most part the language of the younger generation. Expressions that are not used by the younger generation are clearly indicated as such.

Overlapping forms

A consequence of so much variation in vernacular language is that sometimes variants for two different forms overlap. One example of where this occurs is the verbal tense suffix 〜てん (see Sections 5-1 and 5-2). In certain contexts, this marker is equivalent to SJ 〜ている. In other contexts, it is equivalent to the SJ past tense suffix 〜た. Often, the choice between these two is clear, but not always. However, this ambiguity in the grammatical meaning does not cause native speakers any concern at all. They do not worry about it, and neither should you. In these situations, if the speaker needs to be very clear about the intended meaning, then he or she uses SJ instead.

1-2 Stylistic variation

The previous section listed several examples of variants. For each case, the variants were listed in order from the most standard to the most vernacular. The variation seen in those lists ranges along a continuum between standard and vernacular. Recall that VJ is the casual Japanese used with friends and family. It is casual Japanese. In contrast, SJ is formal Japanese. It is useful to think about the standard~vernacular continuum as also being a formal ~casual continuum. As you go about speaking Japanese to others, it is important to speak with an appropriate level of formality. You must not be too casual, but you also must not be too formal either. There are many factors that determine what an appropriate level is. Here are three of them: the social context, the characteristics of the listener, and the characteristics of the speaker.

The social context

The most important factor is without a doubt the social context. How formal is the situation? Formal situations include speaking to strangers (including store staff), answering and asking questions during a university class, and writing emails. In formal situations, use SJ. Casual situations include eating a meal together, going to *karaoke*, and text messaging. In such situations, you should use a more vernacular tone.

The characteristics of the listener

The second most important factor is the characteristics of the person or people that you are talking to, starting with the number of people listening. The greater the number of people that are listening to you, the more formal the situation. You should use SJ when talking to a group of people, but you could use a more casual tone when talking to just one person in the group, even if others are listening.

The next important characteristic of the listener is your relationship with him or her. If the listener is not a member of your family or your friend, then use SJ. Start off speaking in SJ with someone that you have just met. My own personal experience is that Japanese people will ask each other to use a casual tone if they want to build a friendship with that person. However, Japanese people will tend to use a formal tone with any non-native Japanese speaker unless his or her level of Japanese is quite proficient. You can always ask the Japanese person to speak in a casual tone if you prefer.

Another important consideration is hierarchical status. This refers to whether or not a person is superior to you. Japanese culture values hierarchical status more than western cultures do. In Japanese culture, a superior person is someone who has more experience or who is older than you are. Japanese call such people 先輩(せんぱい), which means a person who is senior to you. Use a formal tone when talking with such people. The age gap can be small. University students use a more formal tone with students who are just one year senior, and use a more casual tone with students who are just one year junior.

A student-teacher relationship is always formal from the perspective of the student. Do not use vernacular language with someone who is teaching you. However, a teacher might use a more vernacular tone when addressing a student, particularly if there is a large age difference between them.

The characteristic of the speaker

The last factor is the characteristic of the speaker. Some speakers prefer a more casual tone, others a more formal tone. Generally speaking, men tend to use vernacular language more often

1 The Nature of Vernacular Language

than women do. Although perhaps not as important as the other factors, the characteristic of the speaker is still critical.

What level is appropriate?

So what level of formality is appropriate? It really depends on the above factors. Furthermore, the above factors may interact with each other. For example, imagine that you are on an exchange program and that you are staying with a host family. Your host mother and father are older than you are, so you should speak in a formal tone to them. However, eating dinner together is a casual situation. You should reduce the level of formality while eating together, but increase it again after you finish eating.

Keep in mind that level of formality is a continuum. It is possible to reduce gradually your level of formality over time as you get to know someone better, while still making small adjustments on a case-by-case basis to match the specific social context.

This may seem complicated if you are a beginner level Japanese speaker. A simple strategy that you can use is to imitate the Japanese people around you. If they speak in a casual tone, then you can assume that in that situation it is appropriate to use a casual tone. However, you should really pay attention to Japanese speakers interacting with each other, as native speakers tend to be very formal when speaking with non-native Japanese speakers.

What happens if you use an inappropriately casual tone? Well, no one will be impressed, that is for sure. Native speakers might be amused by your Japanese—Oh look! A foreigner trying to speak the Kansai dialect! In the end, you will leave other people feeling that your Japanese is good, but not great. In order to be considered a great speaker, you must use an appropriate level of formality. However, if your Japanese ability is obviously good enough that you should know better, then your speech could come across as rude. No Japanese person would speak that way, and neither should you. But do not worry as once you become comfortable with VJ, you will be able to easily adjust your level up and down the standard~vernacular continuum. Finally, level of formality is not precise. As long as you are close to an appropriate level, then it is good enough.

1-3 Accommodation

What is accommodation?

Why not just use formal SJ all of the time? This seems like a safe course of action. You certainly will not need to worry about being inappropriately rude. If you are still a beginner level Japanese speaker, then using formal SJ all of the time is fine. However, as you become more proficient, you will need to start adjusting your level of formality. In order to understand why, let us look at some interesting social psychology research on conversation.

Social psychologists have shown that speakers subconsciously influence each other. If one of the conversation participants starts to speak faster and use bigger hand gestures, then the other participants also begin to speak faster and use bigger hand gestures. This influence is called *accommodation,* and speakers are said to accommodate to each other. This means that speakers often imitate each other.

Speakers accommodate to each other in many different ways. Speakers can accommodate how quickly or how loudly they speak. Thus, if one person begins to speak quickly and loudly, then the other participants in the conversation will also. Speakers also repeat words and expressions that were just spoken by others. They even accommodate syntactic patterns such as passive voice. Thus, if one person begins to use passive voice frequently, others will also begin to use passive voice more.

Speakers also accommodate level of formality. If one speaker gradually shifts from a formal tone to a casual tone, then the other participants in the conversation also tend to gradually shift their tone as well. This shift is illustrated by Figure 1-1. This figure

1 The Nature of Vernacular Language

shows an approximation of the degree of formality used by two Japanese speakers during a one-hour-long conversation. The degree of formality was determined by the speaker's copula variants (see Section 3-1, p. 29). If the speaker used です, two points were given; if だ, then one point was given; and if や, then zero points were given. The speaker's formality score is the average score for each five minute period of the interview. Thus, a higher score indicates a more formal tone. As can be seen in the figure, Speaker A first shifts to a more casual style and then speaker B follows. That is, speaker B accommodates to speaker A.

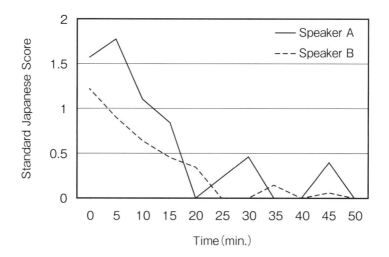

Figure 1-1. Changes in Standard Japanese scores during a 50 minute conversational interview.

What does accommodating do?

The research by social psychologists has shown that speakers accommodate to each other in order to establish a sense of trust and intimacy. If someone speaks in a similar way to you, then you feel closer to that person. Therefore, it is important to accommodate when speaking with friends. By accommodating, you subconsciously build a sense of intimacy.

The opposite effect also happens. If you do not accommodate when speaking with friends, then you psychologically push that person away from you. You convey a feeling of social distance. These effects are subtle, but they are real. For example, if your friends speak to you in a very casual, vernacular style and you use a formal, standard style, then you subconsciously establish social distance, which impedes intimacy.

Proficient non-Japanese students tend to speak in tone that is not vernacular enough when speaking to their Japanese friends and classmates. They tend to use mostly SJ even in a situation in which all of the other Japanese students around them are using only VJ. This lack of accommodation tends to subconsciously push the Japanese students away from the non-Japanese students. As you become more proficient in VJ, pay attention to this. You do not need to use as much vernacular language as the Japanese people around you, although even using a small amount of vernacular language will greatly reduce the negative psychological effects.

Finally, let me warn you that using too much VJ can also have the same negative effect of creating social distance. In order to establish a sense of trust and intimacy with someone, you really must speak similar to the way that he or she does. Remember to accommodate and everything should work out in the end.

2 The Structure of Vernacular Language

2-1 The pressure to speak quickly

This chapter introduces some interesting results from research on the structure of spoken language. Although this chapter may feel more theoretical than the others may, its objective is the same: to help you speak more like a native Japanese person. The underlying theme connecting the different topics is the pressure to speak quickly.

When speakers choose their words during conversation, they tend to use commonly used words and simple grammar. Compare the following two sentences.

◇ The cat that is black and white is mine.
◇ My cat is the black and white one.

The first sentence is grammatically complex (it contains a relative clause); the second sentence is grammatically simple. Speakers tend to prefer simple sentences in conversation. The reason for this preference is that the processing of complex language takes more time than the processing of simple language. In this case, *processing language* means the unconscious mental effort required to recall the meaning of a word or grammatical pattern from your memory.

In general, the amount of time required recalling a word or grammatical pattern in your native language is very small. For example, how long does it take to recall the meaning of a single word that you just read in this sentence? The amount of time is so small that it feels like it is instantaneous, but it is not: In fact, it is approximately one third of a second.

Psycholinguistic research on the time required to process a

word or grammatical pattern has shown that frequently used words and patterns are processed faster. Speakers are forced to reduce their rate of speech if they want to use rare words and complex grammatical patterns. When time is not a concern, then this is not an issue. This is the case of speaking slowly and carefully. This is also the case of writing carefully. Normally, a writer can take as much time as necessary to compose a sentence. However, natural conversation is very different. People tend to speak quickly, and as strange as it sounds, speakers do not want to wait for the delayed brain activity to process rare words and complex grammatical patterns. This requirement to speak quickly results in several interesting characteristics of vernacular language. As you read the remainder of this chapter, keep in mind that these characteristics are unique to vernacular language, and are a consequence of speakers' desire to talk quickly.

2-2 Chaining

The first characteristic of vernacular language introduced in this chapter is *chaining*. In order to understand this concept, let us first review some SJ grammar. In SJ, two short sentences containing verbs can be connected together with the suffix 〜て. Look at the following three examples. The first two examples are two independent sentences. The third example shows the first two sentences connected together by the verbal suffix 〜て.

◇ 朝ご飯を食べた。　　　　　I ate breakfast.
◇ 学校に行った。　　　　　　I went to school.
◇ 朝ご飯を食べて、学校に行った。　I ate breakfast and then I went to school.

The above example shows verbs. Nouns can also be connected together. In such a case, you use the connector で. This で is the conjunctive form of the non-polite SJ copula だ. Here is an example.

◇ 父は医者だ。　　　　　　　　My father is a doctor.
◇ 父は大学の先生だ。　　　　　My father is a university professor.

◇ 父は医者で、大学の先生だ。　My father is a doctor, and a university professor.

な-adjectives follow the same pattern as nouns.

◇ この大学のキャンパスは綺麗だ。　This university campus is pretty.
◇ この大学のキャンパスは静かだ。　This university campus is quiet.
◇ この大学のキャンパスは綺麗で、静かだ。　This university campus is pretty and quiet.

Lastly, い-adjectives are connected by the connector 〜くて, as seen in the following example.

◇ この車は小さい。　　　　　　This car is small.
◇ この車は速い。　　　　　　　This car is fast.
◇ この車は小さくて、速い。　　This car is small and fast.

We now have enough background information to continue. All of the unconnected sentences in the above examples are short and grammatically simple. As pointed out in the introduction to this chapter, speakers prefer simple grammatical patterns to complex grammatical patterns when speaking quickly. In vernacular speech, speakers tend to link together several short sentences with connectors. Furthermore, unlike SJ, the last sentence in the chain often ends in another connector. Here is an actual example taken from the *Corpus of Kansai Vernacular Japanese*. The speaker is a female high school student. Do not worry if you do not understand the contents. Focus on the highlighted parts only. These are connectors. Do you see how the speaker is using them to join one segment after another in the story that she is telling? Look at how the final sentence ends. It ends in a connector.

なんか、この前メールして**て**、今度記念日の日空いてる、なんか、日曜やっ**て**、日曜空いてるって聞いたら、あ、練習試合っ**て**、言われ**て**、え、何かあるん？って言われ**て**、まあそれで怒った、忘れてると思っ**て**。

Now go back to the example sentences at the start of this section, and modify them so that they end in て. By doing that you construct ungrammatical sentences. They are ungrammatical because they no longer have tense. But processing tense takes effort. It is much easier to speak without worrying about tense. This is why speakers often end sentences in て when speaking quickly. The requirement to speak quickly trumps the need to use tense.

2-3 Knowing a few words equals much understanding

As mentioned in the introduction of this chapter, frequently used words are processed faster, and speakers want to talk quickly. Therefore, speakers prefer frequently occurring words and avoid rarer words. This is a feedback loop. The frequently occurring words are preferred by speakers, and so they are used. Because they are often used, they become even more frequent. In contrast, rarer words are avoided, so consequently they are used even less often.

The result of this preference for frequently occurring words is fascinating. However, in order to understand the result you first need to understand the idea of a linguistic morpheme. A morpheme is the smallest part of language that has either lexical or grammatical meaning. For example, the word *eating* consists of two parts: *eat* and *-ing*. Both of these parts have meaning. The verb stem *eat* provides the lexical meaning; the verb suffix -*ing* provides the grammatical meaning (present continuous tense). Similarly, the Japanese phrase 食べている consists of four parts: 食べ, て, い, and る. Again, all of these parts have meaning. In this case, the first part, 食べ, provides the lexical meaning, while the other parts, て+い+る, provide the grammatical meaning. Note that breaking up, for example, 食べ into even smaller parts would result in meaningless parts.

The *Corpus of Kansai Vernacular Japanese* contains about 1.7 million morphemes. These data are made up from approximately 55,000 unique items. This means that in order to understand everything said in daily conversation between native speakers, you need to know over 55,000 morphemes. That is a lot of morphemes! But do not despair: There is good news coming.

How many morphemes do you need to know in order to understand half of everything said in daily conversation? Recall that the most-frequently used morphemes are used a lot. In fact, the most frequently-used morpheme, the 〜て verbal suffix, occurs over 73,000 times in the corpus. That is a large number. In fact, it is 4.3% of the entire data set. In other words, if you learn only one morpheme, then you can understand almost five percent of daily conversation. This leads us to ask the question, how many morphemes does it take to reach 50% of the data? What about 90% of the data? Certainly if you could understand 90% of daily conversation, then that would be a good result. How many morphemes do you need in order to get that far?

Table 2-1 shows the number of morphemes required to understand 10% of the corpus data, and for each 10% interval beyond that. The number of morphemes needed to understand 90% of the conversations is only 2,392 and in order to understand 50% of the conversations you need only 66. Yet, in order to understand almost everything said, you need over 50,000 morphemes. This table really drives home the point that the common morphemes are used very frequently. Also, note that these numbers reflect conversational Japanese. The number of morphemes at each level for written Japanese is much higher.

Proportion Understood	Number of Morphemes	Proportion Understood	Number of Morphemes
10%	4	60%	127
20%	9	70%	269
30%	19	80%	699
40%	36	90%	2,392
50%	66	100%	55,000+

Table 2-1. Number of morphemes needed to understand conversational Japanese.

What are the most frequently used morphemes? Table 2-2 lists the top forty-five most-frequently-used morphemes. Recall that a morpheme is the smallest unit with either lexical or grammatical meaning. However, the list consists almost entirely of grammatical items. Other than the verb する at rank 11, which often has a purely grammatical role, the most frequently occurring item with lexical meaning is the verb 言う at rank 21.

Rank	Item	Rank	Item	Rank	Item
1	て	16	で (part)	31	みたい
2	た	17	も	32	ねん
3	や	18	と	33	を
4	の	19	けど	34	で (conj.)
5	は	20	ん (neg.)	35	思う
6	な	21	言う	36	です
7	に	22	ない	37	まあ
8	が	23	ある	38	人
9	か	24	ね	39	なる
10	だ	25	なんか	40	それ
11	する	26	行く	41	ん (s.f.p.)
12	って	27	もう	42	へん
13	そう	28	うん	43	し
14	から	29	その	44	でも
15	とか	30	る	45	よ

Table 2-2. The most frequently used morphemes and words.

2-4 Morpheme bundles

A morpheme bundle is a sequence of morphemes that frequently occur together. Some examples from English are *have a look at, the end of*, and *I don't know*. Linguists often make a distinction between different types of morpheme bundles such as idioms (*kick the bucket*), collocations (*salt and pepper*), and formulaic expressions (*all of a sudden*). However, in this book all such language is called morpheme bundles.

Two characteristics of morpheme bundles

Morpheme bundles have two important characteristics related to the theme of this chapter, speaking quickly. The first characteristic is that they tend to have only one way of saying them. Consider the idiomatic expression *kick the bucket*, which means to die. You cannot say, 'He kicked a bucket.' Nor can you say, 'He stomped on the bucket.' These sentences no longer have the idiomatic meaning of 'to die.' As another example, consider the expression *salt and pepper*. Have you ever heard anyone say this expression in the reverse order: *pepper and salt*? No, you have not. Why? Morpheme bundles tend to have only one way of saying them.

The second characteristic is related to the first. Because morpheme bundles tend to always occur in the same shape, speakers get used to repeating the expression in that exact same way. An interesting thing happens when we repeat the same action over and over. First, the action becomes ingrained. Second, we tend to make the action as efficient as possible by omitting anything unnecessary. What does this mean? First, the form of the expression tends to crystalize, that is, not change. Second, speakers often omit sounds from the middle of the expression. Consider the morpheme bundle *I don't know*. This is a very common expression in vernacular English. People tend to use this exact combination very frequently. More importantly, people tend to not change the shape of the expression by

25

making the verb past tense *I didn't know*, or by adding more words, for example, *I really don't know*. Fluent English speakers omit the [t] in the middle of the expression. Try saying the expression both with a [t] and without a [t]. Saying it without the [t] is more natural.

Let's consider a Japanese example that illustrates these points: the expression まじで. This expression comes from the な-adjective 真面目 'serious, businesslike, solemn,' and で, which is the conjunctive form of だ. (See Section 2-2, p. 20, for examples of the conjunctive form.) Thus, the expression 真面目で literally means 'it is serious and...' Over time, these morphemes became a morpheme bundle and froze into this shape. The sounds reduced to まじで, and the meaning of 'businesslike' gradually weakened. Nowadays, young people use this expression to mean either 'Are you serious?' or 'Did that really happen?' They also use the expression as a intensifier in the same way as とても 'very.'

This omission of sounds in the middle of expressions occurs frequently in VJ. For example, consider the pronunciation of the phrase 食べている. In natural conversation, no one actually pronounces the い sound. Rather this phrase is pronounced as 食べてる: The い is omitted.

Another example is the pronunciation of おは**よう**ございます 'good morning.' The underlined sound is a long お. However, in natural conversation, people tend to pronounce this sound as a short お.

Section 1.1 explained that one of the characteristics of vernacular language is that it tends to be shorter than standard language. Repetition is one source of reduction. You will see many examples of reduced forms throughout this book, particularly in Chapter 12. Meanwhile, here is a list of the ten most frequently occurring morpheme bundles in the corpus data. After each bundle, a brief explanation or a reference to elsewhere in the book is provided for each morpheme in the bundle.

◇ そう そう そう　　　そう: 4-2
◇ た んや けど　　　　た: past tense; んや: 4-1; けど: 8-1

2 The Structure of Vernacular Language

◇ 〜って いう の は って: 9-2; いう: 'say'; の: 11-4; は: particle
◇ 〜やった かな やった: 4-2; かな: 8-2
◇ 〜みたい な 感じ みたい な: 10-2; 感じ: 10-3
◇ なん て いう ん なん: 'what'; て: 9-2; いう: 'say'; ん: 11-1
◇ そう なん や そう: 4-2; なんや: 4-1
◇ 〜な って 思って な: 8-2; って: 9-2; 思って 'think+て'
◇ 〜ん ちゃう かな んちゃう: 4-4; かな: 8-2
◇ せな あかん せなあかん: 7-2; せ is the verb する

Morpheme bundles and second language acquisition

Morpheme bundles play a very large and important role in language. In fact, much of VJ is composed of morpheme bundles. As pointed out in the previous section, speakers tend to use the same limited set of expressions repeatedly. As your Japanese improves, you also will pick up and use repeatedly a limited set of expressions. That is a natural outcome, so do not worry too much if you feel that you tend to use the same expressions repeatedly. However, in formal contexts and when writing, you should attempt to vary your expressions as much as possible.

The discussion of morpheme bundles ends with a warning: Morpheme bundles sometimes violate the rules of grammar. As mentioned, speakers are so used to saying the morpheme bundle in that way, that the bundle has crystalized in that form. Consider the expression that was just introduced, まじで, which can be used as an adverbial. However, recall that this expression came from a な-adjective 真面目 'serious.' When a な-adjective modifies a verb, it is followed by に, as in the example 静かに話す 'talk quietly.' So naturally the new expression should be まじに, but it is not; it is まじで. Why? The expression まじで has frozen in that form and no longer follows the rules of grammar.

Other examples of morpheme bundles that violate grammar

are highlighted throughout the book, such as the bundle みたいな discussed in Section 10-2 (p. 113). But there are many other examples found throughout the Japanese language. Here is one more example, even though it is not VJ. It is the expression Dictionary form+がよい, which literally means 'doing ～ is fine.' The expression is sometimes seen in anime and manga, and tends to be used with a verb such as 死ぬ 'die,' or 覚悟する 'prepare to die,' as in 死ぬがよい 'It is good for you to die.' The evil boss often uses such an expression just before he or she attacks the hero.

The negative form of よい is よくない. The opposite of よい is 悪い. So if we wanted to say something like 'dying is bad,' then we should be able to say either of the following two sentences.

◇ 死ぬがよくない。
◇ 死ぬが悪い。

However, you cannot. Why? Because Dictionary form+がよい is a morpheme bundle, forever frozen in that shape. Therefore, if you find a strange example of grammar that no one can explain, then it is most likely a morpheme bundle.

3 The Copula

3-1 The basic pattern 〜や

VJ NP や
SJ NP だ

EXAMPLE SENTENCES:

① わたしは学生（がくせい）や。　　　I'm a student.
② 中学校（ちゅうがっこう）ぐらいまでや。　I did it until junior high school.
③ 大阪（おおさか）が好（す）きや。　　I like Osaka.

3-2 Past tense 〜やった

VJ NP やった
SJ NP だった

EXAMPLE SENTENCES:

① あの時（とき）は学生（がくせい）やった。　I was a student at that time.
② 友達（ともだち）が野球部（やきゅうぶ）やった。　My friend was in the baseball club.
③ まあ、大丈夫（だいじょうぶ）やった。　Well, it was fine.

3-3 Conjunction 〜やって

The conjunction is used to connect a noun phrase with a following clause. This concept is explained in detail in Section 2-2 (p. 20).

| VJ | NP やって |
| SJ | NP で |

EXAMPLE SENTENCES:

① 月曜だけやって、他の日はない。 — It's only on Mondays and not on other days.

② たこ焼き好きやって、すしも好きや。 — I like *takoyaki* and I also like *sushi*.

③ 自信がある子やって、何でもできる。 — She's a very confident child, and she's good at everything.

3-4 Negative copula forms

There are three negative forms for the copula: じゃない, ちゃう, and やない. All three have the same meaning, and they are interchangeable. (Recall that having multiple forms for the same meaning is a characteristic of vernacular language.)

Of these three forms, じゃない is by far the most commonly used and it feels very close to SJ. The other two variants feel much more vernacular. The form ちゃう is historically related to the verb 違う 'to be different,' and is used in place of that verb as well as used as the negative copula.

| VJ | NP じゃない |
| SJ | NP ではない |

EXAMPLE SENTENCES:

① お酒が好きじゃない。 — I don't like alcohol.

② どこでもじゃないけど。 — It's not everywhere.

③ 彼は悪い人じゃない。　　　He's not a bad person.

VJ	NP ちゃう
SJ	NP ではない

●●○

EXAMPLE SENTENCES:

④ 今日は金曜日ちゃう。　　　Today is not Friday.
⑤ ぼくの携帯ちゃう。　　　　That's not my cellphone.
⑥ カラオケが嫌いちゃう。　　I don't hate *karaoke*.

VJ	NP やない
SJ	NP ではない

●○○

EXAMPLE SENTENCES:

⑦ 日本人やないと思うけど。　But I think she's not Japanese.
⑧ 冬やないね。夏休みやね。　No, not winter. Summer vacation.
⑨ 恋愛か恋愛やないか分から　I cannot tell if it's love or not.
　ない。

3-5 Negative past tense copula forms

Each of the negative forms introduced in the previous section also has a corresponding past tense form: じゃなかった, ちゃうかった, and やなかった.

VJ	NP じゃなかった
SJ	NP ではなかった

●●●

EXAMPLE SENTENCES:

① 結局、失敗じゃなかった。　　In the end, it was not a failure.
② あれ高三じゃなかった？　　Wasn't that when you were a third year high school student?
③ ずっと学校一緒じゃなかった。　　We didn't always go to the same school.

VJ	NP ちゃうかった
SJ	NP ではなかった

●●○

EXAMPLE SENTENCES:

④ 旅行する家族ちゃうかった。　　We were not a family that traveled.
⑤ レストランちゃうかったか。　　Wasn't it a restaurant?
⑥ あの時まだ幼稚園ちゃうかった。　　I was not yet in kindergarten then.

VJ	NP やなかった
SJ	NP ではなかった

●○○

EXAMPLE SENTENCES:

⑦ 土曜は休みやなかった。　　Saturday was not a day off.
⑧ 釣りは好きやなかった。　　I didn't like fishing.
⑨ あの辺りやなかったかな？　　Wasn't it in that vicinity?

3-6 Polite SJ usage within vernacular language

The usage rates of です and 〜ます forms

From the perspective of vernacular language, not all of the SJ forms are equal. Some forms are used frequently in conversation while some forms are seldom used. In this section, the usage rates of the following eight SJ grammar patterns is examined, based on data from the *Corpus of Vernacular Kansai Japanese*:

◇　です
◇　でした
◇　ではありません
◇　ではありませんでした
◇　ます-form +ます (e.g., 食べます)
◇　ます-form +ました
◇　ます-form +ません
◇　ます-form +ませんでした

These forms are the basic copula and verb patterns for polite SJ, and are learned very early on by Japanese learners. For each of these patterns, the polite SJ form was compared with its vernacular variants. For example, です was compared with だ, や, っす, and す. For each polite SJ pattern, the proportion of tokens that were polite SJ (as opposed to one of the vernacular forms) was calculated. The results are shown in Table 3-1.

	Positive Forms		Negative Forms	
	Form	Usage Rate	Form	Usage Rate
Copula	です	20.30%	ではありません	0.10%
	でした	4.70%	ではありませんでした	0.00%
Verb	verb+ます	4.40%	verb+ません	1.37%
	verb+ました	6.60%	verb+ませんでした	0.27%

Table 3-1. Usage rates for eight polite SJ patterns.

There are two interesting results here. The first is the high rate of usage for です. The second is the extremely low rate of usage for all of the negative forms. These are discussed in turn.

The special status of です

Looking at the positive verb forms in Table 3-1, we can conclude that speakers use polite SJ in conversation about five percent of the time (= the rate of 〜ます). The form でした is also used about five percent of the time. However, the polite SJ copula form です is used much more frequently, or about 20% of the time.

There seem to be two reasons why です is used much more frequently. The first reason is because です occurs in many morpheme bundles (see Section 2-4, p. 25), such as いいですねぇ. Because morpheme bundles are used as is, without any changes, the です form remains in the bundle. This happens even when the speaker is otherwise using a vernacular conversational tone. The following examples of frequently-occurring morpheme bundles contain です. The highlighted part indicates the morpheme bundle. The highlighted parts are worth mastering, as they occur frequently.

EXAMPLE SENTENCES:

① 部屋は物が多いんですか？　　Are there many things in your room?
② 何があるんですか？　　What's there?
③ 住んでる人じゃないですか？　　Isn't she living there?
④ BMWのXシリーズあるじゃないですか？　　So BMW has the X series, right?
⑤ そうなんですか？　　Is that right?
⑥ この前も聞いたんですけど。　　So I heard the other day.
⑦ 質問があるんですけど。　　I have a question.

The second reason why です seems to occur relatively more frequently than other polite SJ forms is because です has a much weaker SJ feeling to it. Because of this weaker SJ feeling, speakers combine です with forms that have a strong vernacular flavor. Following are some examples. (Do not be concerned if you do not understand the grammar, as all of these points are taught in this book.)

EXAMPLE SENTENCES:

⑧	そんなことまで考えとってんですか。	You even take that into consideration?
⑨	全然わからへんですけど。	But I don't get it at all.
⑩	めんどくさいことしよってんです。	Man, you are doing something that is troublesome.
⑪	ほんまに、日本版はあかんのです。	The Japanese version really sucks.

Polite Vernacular Japanese: 〜ないです

The second interesting point from Table 3-1 is that SJ grammatical form 〜ありません almost never occurs. Verb stems followed by the polite SJ ending 〜ます occur approximately five percent of the time in the corpus data. In contrast, verb stems followed by the polite SJ ending 〜ません occur about one percent of the time. Furthermore, the copula form, 〜ではありません occurs about one in a thousand times.

These very low rates of usage mean that if you use these forms, then you are not speaking natural conversational Japanese. Of course, sounding like a textbook is perfectly fine if you are a beginner level speaker, but as you progress, you will reach a point where it will become important to begin sounding more natural.

So what is used instead? The polite negative form in spoken Japanese is 〜ないです. The past tense form inflects the SJ negative form 〜ない for past tense and then adds です.

VJ	NP じゃないです	•••
SJ	NP ではありません	

VJ	NP じゃなかったです	•••
SJ	NP ではありませんでした	

VJ	ない-form+ないです	•••
SJ	ます-form+ません	

VJ	ない-form+なかったです	•••
SJ	ます-form+ませんでした	

EXAMPLE SENTENCES:

⑫ 英語じゃないですか、そんなもの？   Is that sort of thing not English?

⑬ そんなことないです。   No, it's not like that.

⑭ 個人では行かないですか？   Will you not go by yourself?

⑮ あんまり見ないですね。   I don't watch that so often.

⑯ 外車じゃなかったですよ。   It was not a foreign-made car.

⑰ 知らなかったです。   I didn't know that.

Is 〜ない+です correct Japanese?

The combination 〜ない+です may feel like broken Japanese. After all, consider the following two examples:

◇ 食べるです。
◇ 食べないです。

The first sentence is grammatically incorrect. The second sentence is the same as the first sentence except that this time the verb 食べる has been inflected with the verbal negative ending. It is also, strictly speaking, incorrect. However, 〜ない grammatically patterns the same way as an い-adjective. Look at the following example sentences:

⑱ 難しい。 　　　　　　　　　It's difficult.
⑲ 行けない。　　　　　　　　 I cannot go.
⑳ 難しくはないが、したくない。　It's not that it's difficult, but I do not want to do it anyways.
㉑ 行けなくはないが、行きたくない。　It's not that I cannot go, but rather that I don't want to go.

In sentences ⑳ and ㉑, the い-adjective 難しい and the verbal negative suffix 〜ない are both inflected in an identical manner: with く＋は＋ない. Actually, the 〜ない suffix inflects the same as an い-adjective, and grammatically it can be considered as one. Therefore, given that い-adjective+です (for example, 難しいです) is correct grammar, and that 〜ないです is the same pattern, then 〜ないです also seems correct, at least as far as spoken Japanese is concerned.

4 More Copula Expressions

4-1 〜んや and its variants

The patterns introduced in this section are used to soften the tone of the speaker. They are often used when giving a reason or an explanation. They are translated as 'it is just that,' as this expression is used in similar situations.

| VJ | VP んや |
| SJ | VP んだ |

EXAMPLE SENTENCES:

① 結婚してないんや。　　　　It's just that she's not married.
② 今でもやってるんやな？　　You're still doing it even now, right?
③ 彼は体が弱いんや。　　　　It's just that his body is weak.

| VJ | NP なんや |
| SJ | NP なんだ |

EXAMPLE SENTENCES:

④ 実はそれは嘘なんや。　　　Actually, it's a lie.
⑤ 十六歳までなんや？ なるほど。　Just until you're sixteen? That explains it.
⑥ あ、好きなんや。　　　　　Oh, it's that you like it.

The two forms ねや and ねんや are grammatically equivalent to んや, but they both have a very strong regional flavor to them.

| VJ | VP ねや | ●○○ |
| SJ | VP んだ | |

EXAMPLE SENTENCES:

⑦ 子供が「行きたい」と言うねや。   It's just that the kids say that they want to go.

⑧ まー、いっぱい取れたと思うねや。   Well, it's just that I think I got a lot.

⑨ ああいう物じゃないねやけど。   It's just that it's not that sort of thing.

| VJ | VP ねんや | ●○○ |
| SJ | VP んだ | |

EXAMPLE SENTENCES:

⑩ 塾二十年間やってるねんや。   It's just that I have been running a cram school for twenty years.

⑪ 昔はな、重かったねんや。   Well, in the past they were so heavy.

⑫ 会社で弁当注文できるねんや、毎日。   It's just that I can order a lunchbox at work, well like, every day.

4-2 そうや and its variants

This section introduces four phrases that are equivalent to the formal SJ phrase そうですね. Note that そう is a noun, and that そうなんや is the pattern NP なんや introduced in the previous section. The word そう can also be pronounced as a short sound そ (see Section 12-6, p. 147). The expression そうや is often followed by a sentence-final particle such as ね, な, or けど. The せ variant of そう has a very strong vernacular flavor, is only pronounced as a short sound, and tends to be used with the Kansai Japanese sentence-final particles な and で. See Chapter 9 for a discussion of these particles.

VJ	そうや	●●●
VJ	そうなんや	●●○
VJ	そうそうそう	●●●
VJ	せや	●○○
SJ	そうだ	

4-3 Other expressions with や

In general, you can replace the non-polite SJ copula だ with や. Here are some more expressions that use や.

VJ	やから	●●○
SJ	だから	

VJ	やったら	●●●
SJ	だったら	

VJ	なんやかんや	●○○
SJ	なんだかんだ(=あれこれ)	

EXAMPLE SENTENCES:

① 結構無関心やからな。   Because I really don't care.

② 雨降ってきて、やからずっとホテル。   It started to rain, and therefore I stayed in the hotel the whole time.

③ 漫画やったら、ワンピースかな。   If (you talk about) comic books, then One Piece (is a good one).

④ 会社帰りは平日やったら混むし。 — If returning from work on a weekday, then it's crowded.

⑤ 犬は、なんやかんや手かかるな。 — (As for taking care of) a dog, there are many things to do, and it's a lot of work.

4-4 Asking questions

In polite SJ, the question marker か is added on to the end of a sentence to change it into a question. In VJ, the question marker か is used less often. The way of asking a question depends on whether the preceding phrase is a nominal expression or a verbal expression. (See the explanation of these terms in the preface.)

In the case of a verbal expression, の is added on to the end. In VJ, this の particle often reduces to ん. See Chapter 12 for more examples of の reducing to ん.

In the case of a nominal expression, なの is added to the end. Again, の often reduces to ん resulting in なん in place of なの.

VJ	VP の	●●●
VJ	VP ん	●●○
SJ	VP か	

EXAMPLE SENTENCES:

① 月何回ぐらい練習するの？ — About how many times a month do you practice?

② OL言うの？ — Would you say that she's an OL?

③ なんで大阪大学にしたの？ — Why did you choose Osaka University?

④ それは安いん？ — So is that cheap?

⑤ 毎週見てるん？ — Do you watch it every week?

⑥ 先生誰やったん？　　　　　Who was the teacher?

VJ	NP なの	●○○
VJ	NP なん	●●○
SJ	NP ですか	

EXAMPLE SENTENCES:

⑦ ああ、そうなの？ Oh, is that right?
⑧ ご両親の出身はどこなの？ Where are your parents from?
⑨ 週に一日だけ休みなん？ You only have one day off a week?
⑩ 何なん、急に？ What is it? All of a sudden.
⑪ 結婚したい年齢は何歳なん？ At what age do you want to marry?

Besides the two patterns introduced below, another frequently used pattern is to pronounce a sentence with rising intonation. This is indicated with a question mark at the end of the example sentence.

| VJ | Sentence spoken with rising intonation | ●●● |
| SJ | 〜か, 〜ですか | |

EXAMPLE SENTENCES:

⑫ でも可愛くない？ But isn't it cute?
⑬ それいつぐらい？ When about was that?
⑭ 何人？だいたい六十人くらい？ How many people? About sixty people?

4-5 やんか and other expressions of confirmation

This section introduces the following forms used as expressions of confirmation:

◇ やんか
◇ やん
◇ やろ
◇ じゃない
◇ ちゃう
◇ くない

When Japanese speakers are talking to each other, they often use expressions of confirmation. These expressions are used to confirm with the listener that he or she has the same understanding about the topic as the speaker. These expressions add a tag-like question onto the end of the utterance, similar to the English tag questions 'isn't it?' and 'don't you think?' These forms tend to be spoken with rising intonation to indicate their question-like nature, and may be followed with a VJ question marker such as の or ん.

These expressions have two-closely related meanings. Which meaning is intended really depends on the context, and the intonation used by the speaker. The first use is similar to the SJ expression で しょうね when spoken with rising intonation, as if asking a question. In this case, the speaker is asking the listener to confirm what the speaker said. The listener normally responds with a short word such as うん. When the conversation is in SJ then the speakers use はい. Both うん and はい indicate that the listener agrees. The expressions じゃない and ちゃう tend to be only used in this way, as expressions confirming agreement.

The second usage is the same as the grammar pattern NPん や (see Section 4-1, p. 39), which is used to soften an assertion. Similar to the expressions introduced in that section, these expressions are also preceded by one of the softener particles ん, な

4 More Copula Expressions

ん, ね, or ねん. Of these, the particles ね and ねん have a strong VJ flavor to them, and therefore they are not used with じゃない. The particles ね and ねん are not used often, but some example sentences containing them have been included for the sake of completeness. All four of the softener particles are used before a VJ form such as や, やんか, やん, and やろ.

Note that expression やんか is historically related to the expression やないか, and that the SJ form of やないか is じゃないか.

One group of expressions, those that end in やない, have been intentionally left out of this section. They pattern the same as the those ending in じゃない.

Finally, note that くない only follows a verb. It does not follow a noun or an adjective.

VJ	NP やんか, NP なんやんか	●●●
VJ	VP やんか, VP んやんか	●●●
SJ	NP でしょう, VP でしょう, NP なんでしょう, VP んでしょう	

EXAMPLE SENTENCES:

① 学校でカップヌードルとか売ってるやんか。 — So, they sell Cup Noodle at school, right?

② 竹山先生やったやんか、担任が。 — Well, my homeroom teacher was Mr. Takeyama.

③ わたしはどうでもいいやんか。 — So I'm ok with whatever.

④ おじいちゃんは大阪なんやんか。 — Well, my grandfather's from Osaka.

⑤ 親に内緒やねんやんか、付き合ってることは。 — I'm keeping the fact that I'm dating a secret from my parents.

VJ	NP やん, NP なんやん	●●○
VJ	VP やん, VP んやん	●●○
SJ	NP でしょう, VP でしょう, NP なんでしょう, VP んでしょう	

EXAMPLE SENTENCES:

⑥ 周りみんな標準語やん？　Everyone around you is Standard Japanese, right?

⑦ 考えて見れば日本もそうやん。　Well, if you think about it, then Japan is the same.

⑧ 明日の準備とか、朝も早いやん。　Well, on days when I have something like tomorrow's preparation, the mornings are early.

⑨ 絶対あると思うねやん。　Well it's just that I think for sure there's that.

[VJ] NP やろ, NP なんやろ	•••
[VJ] VP やろ, VP んやろ	•••
[SJ] NP でしょう, VP でしょう, NP なんでしょう, VP んでしょう	

EXAMPLE SENTENCES:

⑩ 日曜日もある。ひどいやろ？　Even on Sundays too. Brutal, isn't it?

⑪ どうなってるんやろ？　So what most likely happened?

⑫ 分かるやろ？　You understand, right?

⑬ まだ最後まで見てへんねやろ？　You still haven't watched that movie all the way to the end, have you?

[VJ] NP じゃない, VPじゃない	•••
[VJ] VP んじゃない	•••
[VJ] NP なんじゃない	•••
[SJ] NP ではないですか, VP んではないですか, NP なんではないですか	

EXAMPLE SENTENCES:

⑭ あれ初めてじゃない？ — That's the first time, right? (Note that 初めて is used as a noun. Example: 初めての恋 'my first time falling in love')

⑮ そうゆう意味じゃない？ — That's what you mean, right?

⑯ いいじゃないの？ — Well, isn't it just fine?

⑰ 今一番充実してるんじゃないかな。 — Well, perhaps (my life) right now is the most fulfilling.

⑱ 社会人もそうなんじゃないん？ — Well, working people are also the same, right?

⑲ わりと、いい方なんじゃない？ — Relatively, that was the better way, don't you think?

VJ	NP ちゃう	●●○
VJ	VP んちゃう	●●○
VJ	NP なんちゃう	●●○
SJ	NP ではないですか, VP んではないですか, NP なんではないですか	

EXAMPLE SENTENCES:

⑳ 先にフランス語じゃなくて、英語ちゃう？ — First (you must learn) English, not French, don't you think?

㉑ 野球見るの好きちゃう？ — You like to watch baseball, right?

㉒ 付き合ったらええんちゃうん？ — You should start dating, don't you think?

㉓ 三百円ぐらいやったんちゃう？ — It was about 300 yen, right?

㉔ 歳の差なんちゃう？ — It is because of the age difference, right?

㉕ 田中はできるんちゃう？ — Tanaka can do it, right?

|VJ| verb くない？
|SJ| verb んではないですか

●○○

EXAMPLE SENTENCES:

㉖ 借りてもお金かかるくない？   Even if you just rent it, it still costs money, right?

㉗ おしゃれなカフェいっぱいあるくない？   There are lots of stylish coffee shops, don't you think?

㉘ 二十歳でもあかんくない？   Even if you are twenty, it's still not a good thing to do, don't you think?

4-6 A youthful variant 〜っす

This is a vernacular variant of the SJ copula です used by the younger generation throughout Japan. Like many innovative forms used by youth, many older people see this form as broken Japanese. Some older people dislike when young people use it, and they may become angry if you use this form with them. In general, you should be using SJ with people who are older than you are. However, if you are in a situation in which using VJ with an older person is appropriate, then you are better off using the Kansai form や. No one dislikes や. The forms introduced in this section are used by youth when speaking to other youth in a semi-polite way. For example, if you are university student, then you could use these forms with other students who are your 先輩.

Since this form is based on SJ です, it is used in combination with other SJ forms. For example, it is used with the SJ sentence-final particles ね or よ, and not with the Kansai dialect sentence-final particles ねん or で.

The form っす may optionally be pronounced as す. Recall from

Chapter 1 that one of the characteristics of VJ is multiple ways to say the same thing. The す variant is rare. There is, however, one case in which only the す variant is used: after the ん in the expression VP+ん+す. This pattern is the same as 〜んや, 〜んだ, and 〜んです. The first of those, 〜んや, was discussed earlier in this chapter. The pattern ん+です is a frequently occurring morpheme bundle. Again, recall from Chapter 1 that frequently occurring morpheme bundles tend to shorten, and so ん+っす has shortened to ん+す.

VJ	〜っす, す	●○○
SJ	です	
VJ	〜ん+す	●○○
SJ	〜ん+です	

EXAMPLE SENTENCES:

① そうっすね。 That's right, isn't it?
② ポルシェかっこいいすね。 The Porsche's stylish, isn't it?
③ 無理っすよね。 It's useless, isn't it?
④ 五年半っすよ。 It's five and a half years.
⑤ いいんすよ。 It's fine.
⑥ そんなのがあるんすね。 There are ones like that, aren't there?

There is also a vernacular version of でしょう. Again, there are two variants: っしょ, and しょ. Similar to っす, only しょ occurs after the ん in ん+でしょう.

VJ	〜っしょ, しょ	●○○
SJ	でしょう	
VJ	〜ん+しょ	●○○
SJ	〜ん+でしょう	

EXAMPLE SENTENCES:

⑦ お金ないっしょ。 　　　　　You don't have any money, right?
⑧ おかしいっしょ？ 　　　　　That's strange, isn't it?
⑨ 全然仲いいっしょ。 　　　　They get along very well, right?
⑩ おばあちゃんしょ？ 　　　　It's grandmother, isn't it?
⑪ 何っしょね？ 　　　　　　　What is it?
⑫ 新聞見たら分かるんしょ。 　If you read the newspaper, you'd probably know that.

5 Basic Verb Forms

5-1 Present continuous tense forms

The present continuous tense form in SJ is て-form+て+いる, as in 食べている 'eating.' This section introduces four VJ variants for 〜て+いる: 〜とる, 〜てん, 〜とん, and 〜とう.

The VJ variant for the verb いる is おる. Consequently, the VJ variant for the SJ form 〜て+いる is based on the form 〜て+おる. These two morphemes have combined to produce 〜とる. This form attaches to the て-form of a verb. For example, the VJ variant of the SJ phrase 行っている is 行っとる. If the verb uses 〜で instead of 〜て (飲んで, 泳いで, etc.), then 〜とる becomes 〜どる. This point about the alternation between /t/ and /d/ holds for all of the forms introduced in this section.

| VJ | て-form+とる, て-form+どる | ••• |
| SJ | て-form+ている | |

EXAMPLE SENTENCES:

① 結婚しとるね。　　　　　He's married, right?
② 覚えとるよ。　　　　　　I remember it.
③ 日曜日はボーッとしとる。　I'm sitting around daydreaming on Sundays.
④ 百歳なっとるな。　　　　He has become 100 years old.
⑤ いつも洋子と遊んどる。　I'm always hanging out with Yoko.

In order to understand this next pattern, you should first read about the sound pattern る to ん introduced in Section 11-7 (p. 135). This next pattern also begins with the SJ form 〜ている. In spoken language, the form 〜ている is almost always pronounced as 〜てる. As explained in Section 11-7, る changes to ん before another nasal sound (the sounds m and n). A commonly-occurring environment for this sound change is a verb-final る followed by a sentence-final particle beginning with a nasal sound, such as ねん, の, and ん. Thus, for example, 〜てる+ねん changes to 〜てんねん.

The sentence-final particle ん involves another change: two ん in a row reduce to one. Therefore 〜てる+ん becomes 〜てん+ん, which in turn reduces to just 〜てん.

Technically the sentence-final particles ね and な also start with a nasal sound, and therefore it is the correct environment for the change. However, ね has a much more SJ feel to it, and so the combination 〜て+ん+ね is very rare. In contrast, な feels less standard, and 〜て+ん+な occurs frequently. However, this combination tends to indicate the past tense, so 〜てんな is introduced in the next section.

You may be surprised to learn that 〜てん has two grammatical meanings: present continuous tense and past tense. In Section 1-1 (p. 9), 〜てん was given as an example of an overlapping form. Remember that the grammatical ambiguity resulting from this form having two grammatical meanings is not worth worrying about, and if needed, you can always use SJ. However, having said that, 〜てん does show a strong tendency to indicate the present continuous tense when followed by the particles ねん and の, and to indicate the past tense when followed by the particle な or when not followed by anything. That is how 〜てん is introduced in the following example sentences.

There is one more form: 〜とん. This is a combination of 〜て+おる+ん. Similar to 〜てん, this form can indicate both present continuous tense and past tense. Again similar to 〜てん, 〜とん has a strong tendency to indicate the present continuous tense when followed by the particles ねん and の, and to indicate the past tense when followed by the particle な or when not followed by anything.

5 Basic Verb Forms

| VJ | て-form+てん, て-form+でん | ●●● |
| SJ | て-form+ている, て-form+でいる | |

| VJ | て-form+とん, て-form+どん | ●○○ |
| SJ | て-form+ている, て-form+でいる | |

EXAMPLE SENTENCES:

⑥ もう寝ようかと思ったら寝てんねん。 — When I thought that it was time to sleep, she was already asleep!

⑦ うちは健ちゃんて呼んでんねんけどな。 — I call him, "Ken-chan." (The て equals と. See Section 9-1.)

⑧ 今、頑張ってんねん。 — These days, I'm trying my hardest.

⑨ 話をしたり聞いたりしてんねん。 — I'm talking and listening.

⑩ 何年行っとんねん？ — For how many years have you been going there?

⑪ まだテーブルの上に置いとんねん。 — It's still on the table.

⑫ 昔からそこに住んでんの？ — Have you been living there since the past (=for a long time)?

⑬ お父さん仕事何してんの？ — What does your father do for a living?

Another form of the vernacular variant of SJ 〜ている is 〜とう. This is a further reduction of the vernacular form 〜とる. This form has a strong vernacular feeling to it.

| VJ | て-form+とう, て-form+どう | ●○○ |
| SJ | て-form+ている, て-form+でいる | |

EXAMPLE SENTENCES:

⑭ 近いところがええかとは思っとう。 — I'm thinking that somewhere close is good.

⑮ 空手やっとうけど、あまり強くない。 — I'm learning *karate*, but I'm not so strong.

⑯ これぐらい人来とうかな。 — Wow, have so many people really come?

⑰ 芦屋ゆうたらめっちゃお金持ちが住んどうな。 — As for Ashiya district, there are lots of rich people living there.

Some verbs that indicate an ongoing state naturally take the form て-form+て+いる, even though their English equivalents do not use the *-ing* form of the verb. The following are some examples of such expressions:

◇ 彼は結婚している。 — He's married.
◇ 覚えているよ。 — I remember.
◇ それを知っている。 — I know that.
◇ あの二人はとても似ている。 — Those two are very similar.

Section 2-2 (p. 20) introduced the concept of chaining. In such a case, verbs are connected together with the suffix 〜て. The verbs indicating state, such as those just introduced, can also be linked to a following predicate in the same manner. In this case, the verb form becomes て-form+て+いる. This combination is SJ. There is one corresponding VJ form: て-form+とって.

| VJ | て-form+とって, て-form+どって | ••• |
| SJ | て-form+ていて, て-form+でいて | |

EXAMPLE SENTENCES:

⑱ 前から知っとって、ってこと？ So, you're saying that you already knew that?

⑲ 友達住んどって、もう三年くらいロンドン住んどって。 My friend lives in London, and he has been living there for three years now.

5-2 Past tense forms

As mentioned in the previous section, one way of expressing the past tense in VJ is with the morpheme ～てん. A similar form, which looks more like SJ ～た, is ～たん. This form is historically derived from ～た+の. A third form is based on the form ～て plus the past tense of the verb おる. It is ～とん. Thus, there are in total three different VJ morphemes that correspond to the SJ past tense marker ～た: ～てん, ～たん, and ～とん.

Of these, ～てん is the most frequently used. The form ～とん is rarely used, and ～たん is in between.

VJ	て-form+てん, て-form+でん	●●●
VJ	て-form+たん, て-form+だん	●●○
VJ	て-form+とん, て-form+どん	●○○
SJ	て-form+た, て-form+だ	

EXAMPLE SENTENCES:

① 簿記も一応勉強してんな。 I briefly studied bookkeeping.
② 一応、恋愛はしててんな。 I was in love (with him) for a bit.
③ どこ行ったん？ Where did you go?
④ 香港行ったん、俺、高一の時。 I went to Hong Kong when I was a first year high school student.

⑤ 十時なっとんか思った。 I thought, "Has it become 10 o'clock?"
⑥ 地元でやろう思っとん。 I thought I would just do it locally.

There is also one form that corresponds to the SJ pattern て-form+て+いる. It is て-form+とった.

| VJ | て-form+とった, て-form+どった | ••• |
| SJ | て-form+ていた, て-form+でいた | |

EXAMPLE SENTENCES:

⑦ ああ、忘れとった。 Oh, I forgot that.
⑧ ドラマめっちゃ見とった。 I watched lots of television drama shows.
⑨ 小学校のとき友達とは何して遊んどったん？ What did you do with your friends when you were in primary school?
⑩ おばあちゃんといっしょに住んどったんやけど。 I was living with my grandmother.

You should be able to see the parallel patterns between the forms introduced in Section 5-1 and the forms introduced in Section 5-2. Table 5-1 summarizes the forms presented in these two sections. Note the close relationship between SJ forms and the VJ forms base on 〜おる.

5 Basic Verb Forms

	Present Tense			Past Tense		
SJ	VJ	SFP	SJ	VJ	SFP	
〜ている	〜てん 〜たん 〜とん	+ ねん の	〜た	〜てん 〜たん 〜とん	+	な (or none)
〜ている	〜とる 〜とう	(any)				
〜ていて	〜とって	--	〜ていた	〜とった	(any)	

Table 5-1. The commonly occurring verbal tense endings. SFP = sentence-final particle.

5-3 Command forms

The Vernacular Kansai Japanese command form is based on the SJ command form that ends in 〜なさい. Inflect the verb stem for the verb ending 〜なさい, but do not add the ending. For example, in VJ, the command form 食べなさい 'Eat!' is just 食べ.

The command form is often followed by や, as in the example 食べや. In this case, や acts as a sentence-final particle, not the VJ copula.

The command form is also often used with the SJ sentence-final particle よ. This is in spite of the SJ flavor of this particle. In this case, our example of 食べなさい becomes 食べよ.

If the command form ends up being only one sound long (for example, SJ 見なさい becomes 見 in VJ), then the vowel is optionally lengthened. In this case, 見 is optionally realized as 見い.

The irregular verb する has two forms: せ(え) and し(い). The brackets indicate the optional lengthening of the vowel. The irregular verb 来る has only one form: 来(い).

The form verb stem+てみ(い) is the command form of the SJ grammar 〜てみる. This pattern literally means 'do and see (what happens).' It requests the listener to try and do something, or to do something and see what happens.

57

VJ	ます-form
SJ	ます-form+なさい

●●○

EXAMPLE SENTENCES:

① ヨーロッパはいいよ。行き。 Europe is great. Go there!
② 洗濯物ちゃんと出しや。 Put out the laundry!
③ そこ見いや。 Look there!
④ 自分で決め。 Decide by yourself!
⑤ 買ってんからせえよ。 You bought it, so do it!
⑥ そうしいよ。 Do that!
⑦ 体の弱い人は前に出て来い。 People who are weak come to the front.
⑧ もうなんでも来い。 Bring it on! Anything at all!
⑨ 美味しいから食べてみ。 It's delicious, so try it!

5-4 The potential form: ら -dropping

The SJ potential and passive verbal suffix is ない-form+れ+る for Group I verbs, and ない-form+られ+る for Group II verbs. In VJ, the ら sound of the 〜られ〜 morpheme used with Group II verbs is often omitted.

VJ	Group II verb ない-form+れ+る
SJ	ない-form+られ+る

●●●

EXAMPLE SENTENCES:

① 鍵開けれへんかった。 I couldn't open the lock.
② 手に入れれへんかった。 I was unable to get my hands on one.

③ タバコ止めれたらすごく嬉しいんやけれども。

It's just that if I can quit smoking then I will be happy.

④ 自分がその人を見極めれた時に決めたいかな。

I want to decide after I'm able to get a clear picture of what type of person he is.

⑤ 仕事やっとって、なんかやりがいある仕事、それをまあ二十五、六までに見つけれたらええな。

You do your work, you know, like a job worth doing, well, it's awesome if you can find that before you are twenty-five or six.

⑥ 貧しい人に、なんか幸せちょっとでも与えれたかなあ思って、嬉しいな。

I'm happy since I was able to provide poor people with some happiness.

5-5 The causative form

The SJ causative verbal pattern is ない-form+せ+る for Group I verbs, and ない-form+させ+る for Group II verbs. In VJ, these forms may be shortened to ない-form+す for Group I verbs, and ない-form+さす for Group II forms. The shortened form inflects as a Group I verb. Table 12-1 lists several commonly occurring verbs and their VJ causative forms.

Dictionary Form	Meaning	SJ Causative	VJ Causative
行く	'to go'	行かせる	いかす
会う	'to meet'	会わせる	あわす
話す	'to speak'	話させる	はなさす
食べる	'to eat'	食べさせる	たべさす
する	'to do'	させる	さす
来る	'to come'	来させる	こさす

Table 5-2. A list of commonly occurring vernacular causative forms

The form ～さす is often combined with the verb もらう, resulting in ～さしてもらう. The literal translation of this expression is 'be allowed to do,' but in most cases, the speaker does not imply that permission was requested or granted. Rather, this form indicates that the speaker was given an opportunity or the means to do something and shows respect towards those who provided the opportunity or means. Unfortunately, it is very difficult to capture such a nuance in English, and the English translations of the example sentences are only approximations. Nevertheless, ～さしてもらう is a very useful phrase, and you should make an effort to use it in conversational Japanese.

[VJ]	Group I verb ない-form+す	•••
[VJ]	Group II verb ない-form+さす	•••
[SJ]	Group I verb ない-form+せる	
[SJ]	Group II verb ない-form+される	

EXAMPLE SENTENCES:

① お父さんにも少し食べさす。 — I'll make father eat a bit.

② 妹三人も写っていた写真を見さしてもらいましたわ。 — I was shown a picture of his three younger sisters.

③ 卓球さしてもらったり、カラオケ行かしてもらったりしとります。 — I'm doing things like playing ping pong and going to *karaoke*.

④ その体験をさしてあげることも大事かなと思う。 — I think it's important that (I let) you have such an experience.

⑤ 気持ち切り替えささなあかんな。 — I must make someone switch their mood (and become happy).

6 The Verbal Negative Suffixes

The verbal negative suffix 〜へん is one of the most conspicuous characteristics of Vernacular Kansai Japanese. It is used not only in the Kansai region, but also in the immediate vicinity of Kansai. Furthermore, television personalities such as comedians from the Kansai area use it on television, so everyone in Japan is at least familiar with it as a marker of Kansai Japanese.

However, 〜へん is only one suffix in a set of verbal negative suffixes. In fact, Japanese speakers use four different suffixes in conversation: 〜へん, 〜ひん, 〜ん, and the SJ variant 〜ない. Learners of Japanese may feel overwhelmed by the seemingly confusing nature of the way that these suffixes are used. The choice between the variants seems to be random, and for older Japanese speakers it is somewhat random.

However, languages are highly organized systems, and Japanese is no exception. The source of the randomness comes from the fact that the verbal negative system in Vernacular Kansai Japanese is currently undergoing change from an older, obsolete system to a newer system. Furthermore, the new system shows a very simple, highly organized pattern. This pattern is introduced in the next section.

As you learn the pattern in the next section, keep in mind that only the youngest Japanese speakers follow the pattern most of the time, and even then they do not use it consistently. But this inconsistency is not a problem. Recall from Chapter 1 that one of the characteristics of VJ is its multiple ways of saying the same thing, and the negative suffix is an excellent example of this.

Another source of seeming randomness is the fact that some of the variants closely follow a pattern while others do not. For example, according to the basic pattern introduced in Section 6-1 (p. 62), the 〜へん suffix follows verb stems ending in え, and the 〜ひん suffix follows verbs ending in い. However, the 〜へん suffix can be used after a verb ending in い, but the 〜ひん suffix cannot be used after a verb ending in え. Rather the 〜ひん suffix strictly follows the basic pattern. Instead of worrying about these alternative patterns, focus on the basic pattern. In this way, you will not accidentally produce a strange verb-suffix combination.

6-1 The basic pattern: Group I and Group II verbs

The choice of the verbal negative suffix depends on the vowel that comes immediately before the verbal negative suffix. Here is the pattern.

> If **a**, then 〜ん
> If **e**, then 〜へん
> If **i**, then 〜ひん

In order to determine the vowel, inflect the verb stem for the SJ negative suffix 〜ない. The vowel referred to here is the one that comes immediately before the な sound. For example, the negative form of 行く is 行かない, and the vowel immediately before ない is **a**. Similarly, the negative form of 食べる is 食べない, and in this case the vowel immediately before ない is **e**. Therefore the VJ form of 行かない is 行かん, and the VJ form of 食べない is 食べへん.

VJ	ない-form ending in a+ん	•••
VJ	ない-form ending in e+へん	•••
VJ	ない-form ending in i+ひん	•••
SJ	ない-form+ない	

EXAMPLE SENTENCES:

① なんでか知らんけど。　　I don't know why.
② だから男しかおらん。　　Therefore, there were only males.

③ 外で遊ぶのなかなか見かけへんな。   I almost never see them outside playing.

④ あんまり食べへん。   I don't eat so much.

⑤ 仕事ができひんようになった。   It became so that I could no longer work.

⑥ 言葉が通じひん。   I couldn't understand the language.

The basic pattern describes the cases in which the negative suffix immediately follows the verb stem. The same pattern is also followed when a morpheme such as 〜て or 〜られ intervenes between the verb stem and the verbal negative suffix. In this case also, the verbal negative suffix is chosen based on the vowel that immediately precedes the verbal negative suffix. For example, the VJ negative form of the expression 食べている is 食べてへん, as the vowel immediately before the verbal negative suffix (in this case, へん) is the **e** vowel of て.

Following are several examples of negated verbal forms that contain an intervening morpheme.

EXAMPLE SENTENCES:

⑦ なにもしてへん。   I'm not doing anything!

⑧ 今年三回しか行ってへんの？   Have you only been there three times this year?

⑨ 英語が喋られへん。   I cannot speak English.

⑩ パソコン、一切使えへんねん。   I cannot use a personal computer at all.

⑪ 無理やり変化させへん。   I'm not going to force her to change.

⑫ 百本入れるまで終わらせてもらわれへんねん。   So for example, we were not allowed to finish practice until we got in 100 serves.

A generational gap in the usage of the basic pattern

As mentioned above, Japanese speakers show a large amount of variation in their choice of the negative suffix. Because the community as a whole is gradually shifting towards the above pattern, the age of the speaker is important. Older speakers show more variation, whereas younger speakers tend to use the basic pattern. Figure 6-1 shows the proportion of the negative suffixes that follow the basic pattern, by age group. From this figure you can see that it is important to follow the basic pattern, but you must also be able to understand others when they do not follow the pattern. Other than two sets of exceptional forms, all of the example sentences for this chapter follow the basic pattern. The first set of exceptional forms are some of the negative forms for the two irregular verbs する and 来る introduced in Section 6-3 (p. 65). The second set of exceptional forms are Group I plus へん. This pattern is still quite common, even among the younger speakers. See Section 6-8 (p. 72) for further discussion.

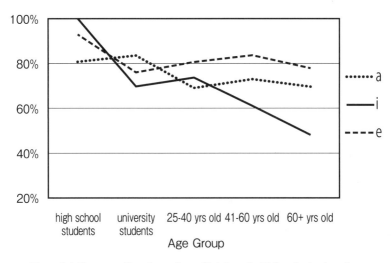

Figure 6-1. The proportion of negative suffix tokens that follow the basic pattern, by age group and preceding vowel.

6-2 Lengthening of Group II verbs

The verb stems of certain Group II verbs are pronounced with a long sound when followed by the negative suffixes 〜へん and 〜ひん. This lengthening only happens when the verb stem is written with a single hiragana sound. For example, the verb stem of the verb 見る is 見. This is written in hiragana as み—a single hiragana sound. This sound is lengthened to みい before the verbal negative suffix, producing the form 見いひん.

VJ	Group II verb ない-form+long sound+へん	●○○
VJ	Group II verb ない-form+long sound+ひん	●○○
SJ	ない-form+ない	

EXAMPLE SENTENCES:

① あー、もう寝えへんかな？ Ahh, how about going to bed?

② これは着いひんやろう。 You're not going to wear this, right?

③ 障がい者を大人として見るか見いひんか、という問題や。 It's a matter of whether or not you view a person with a disability as an adult or not.

④ 先輩いいひんの？ (negative of いる) Are there none of your *sempai* there?

6-3 Irregular verbs

This section covers the negative forms for the two irregular verbs する and 来る. You will not be surprised to hear that there are multiple variants used for the negative forms for these verbs. However, while all of the forms listed below are used, some forms are used much more frequently than others. Beginner level readers should focus on only the most common forms for each verb.

When inflected for a following verbal negative suffix, the stems

65

for these two verbs have only a single hiragana sound. As explained in the previous section, in such a case that single hiragana sound is lengthened. Thus, the negative form of 見る is 見いひん. The same vowel lengthening phenomenon also occurs with the negative forms of the verbs する and 来る. However, lengthening does not occur before 〜ん. A good guideline for the irregular verbs is that their VJ negative forms tend to have an even number of hiragana sounds.

VJ	せん, せえへん	●●●
VJ	しいひん	●●○
VJ	せやへん、しやひん、しやへん	●○○
SJ	しない	

VJ	来ん、来えへん、来おへん	●●●
VJ	来いひん	●●○
VJ	来やへん、来やひん、来やへん	●○○
SJ	来ない	

EXAMPLE SENTENCES:

① バイト結局せんようになった。 — In the end, it turns out that I'm not going to do a part-time job.

② あんたゲームはせえへんよな？ — You don't play video games, right?

③ 勉強しかしいひんよ。 — I did nothing but studying.

④ もう仲のいい子以外は来ん。 — Only those kids that get along well together come.

⑤ 何やっけ、名前出て来えへんな。 — What was it? I cannot recall his name.

⑥ 帰って来やへんのは残念やった。 — It was too bad that she's not going to come back.

Besides the verbs する and 来る, one more irregular verb needs

to mentioned in this section: ある. The VJ negative form of ある is あらへん. This form is sometimes produced with vowel harmony (see Section 6-8, p. 72): あれへん. However, you will most likely not hear either of these forms used by Japanese speakers, as they have now been completely replaced by the SJ form ない among the middle-aged and younger generations. So unless you want to sound like an elderly man or woman, you should only use the SJ form. For the sake of completeness, here are some examples, but they were produced by elderly speakers.

VJ	あらへん, あれへん	●○○
SJ	ない	

EXAMPLE SENTENCES:

⑦ 今はそんなことあらへんやん。   You don't see that sort of thing nowadays.

⑧ アメリカは公共交通機関が基本的にあれへん。   Basically, the United States doesn't have a public transit system.

⑨ あいつはしょうもあれへんな。   He's without hope (=useless).

6-4 The past tense

The verbal past tense also follows the basic pattern.

VJ	ない-form ending in **a**+んかった	●●●
VJ	ない-form ending in **e**+へんかった	●●●
VJ	ない-form ending in **i**+ひんかった	●●●
SJ	ない-form+なかった	

EXAMPLE SENTENCES:

① お父さんおらんかった。　Father was not home.
② 口に合わんかったな。　I didn't like the flavor.
③ 英語喋れへんかった。　I couldn't speak English.
④ 最近行ってへんかった。　I haven't gone recently.
⑤ 四年か五年、子供できひんかった。　For four or five years, I couldn't make a child (=get pregnant).
⑥ その当時はなんも感じひんかった。　At that time, I didn't feel anything.

6-5 The conditionals 〜と, 〜たら

SJ has four conditionals: 〜と, 〜たら, 〜れば, and 〜なら. Of these, only 〜と and 〜たら are used with the VJ negative suffixes introduced in this chapter. Of the other two, 〜れば is used in conversation, but it is used rarely and only in the SJ form 〜なければ. This leaves 〜なら. Unfortunately, this one is a source of confusion. The combination ん+なら occurs in VJ, but in this case ん is almost never a negative marker. See Section 12-5 (p. 146) for the form んなら as an abbreviation of それなら, and Section 11-7 (p. 135) for んなら as a VJ variant of a verb stem ending in る+なら.

VJ	ない-form+んと, ない-form+んかったら	●●○
VJ	ない-form+へんと, ない-form+へんかったら	●●○
VJ	ない-form+ひんと, ない-form+ひんかったら	●●○
SJ	ない-form+ないと, ない-form+なかったら	

EXAMPLE SENTENCES:

① 毎日やらんと下手になる？　If you don't do it every day, then will you become poor at doing it?

② 気合わんかったらすぐ別れるけど。 — But if a couple does not get along, then they will break up quickly.

③ 続いてへんと困るわ。 — I'll be upset if it's not continuing.

④ 半年せえへんかったら忘れる。 — If you don't do it for half a year then you forget how.

⑤ もうできひんと落ちこぼれる。 — If you cannot do it now then you'll fall behind.

⑥ 自分だけできひんかったら嫌やんか。 — It's just that if I'm the only one who cannot do it, then I get upset.

6-6 The conjunctive forms ～んくて, ～へんくて

The conjunctive form joins two verbs, of which the first has been inflected with the verbal negative suffix. There is a tendency to only use ～ん+くて, and to not use the two other negative suffix forms seen in the basic pattern. The forms ～へんくて and ～ひんくて do occur, but infrequently. Only the most common form is introduced in the example sentences. However, there is one case where ～へんくて must occur. The verbal suffix ～て cannot be followed by ～ん, only by ～へん as in the expression 食べてへん (the SJ form is 食べてない 'not eating'). In this case, the conjunctive form becomes ～へんくて, as in the example 食べてへんくて.

| VJ | ない-form+んくて | ●●● |
| SJ | ない-form+なくて | |

| VJ | て-form+へんくて | ●●○ |
| SJ | て-form+て+なくて | |

EXAMPLE SENTENCES:

① なんか喋らんくて、「えー、どうしよう」と思った。 — I didn't talk at all, and I thought, "Ahh, what am I going to do?"

② スケジュールが合わんくて、行ってないな。 — It didn't match my schedule, and I have not been going.

③ 場所覚えてへんくて、分からん。 — I don't remember the place, and I don't know.

④ その子行かんくて、私行けた。 — That girl couldn't go, and so I was able to go.

⑤ 全然パソコンないから見てへんくて。 — I don't have a computer at all, so I have not been watching it, and…

6-7 Potential negative

The SJ potential negative suffix for Group I verbs is 〜えない, and for Group II verbs is for 〜られない. Thus, the SJ expressions for 'cannot go' and 'cannot eat' are 行けない and 食べられない respectively.

As has been repeated throughout this book, one of the characteristics of vernacular language is that there are multiple ways of saying the same thing. The VJ potential negative is a typical example of this, as there are two commonly used ways for both Group I and Group II verbs. The two suffixes used with Group I verbs are 〜あれへん and 〜えへん. The two suffixes used with Group II verbs are 〜られへん and 〜れへん. Thus, the vernacular expressions for 'cannot go' are 行かれへん and 行けへん. The expressions for 'cannot eat' are 食べられへん and 食べれへん. Note that the vowel immediately before 〜へん is え, and therefore these forms follow the basic pattern introduced in Section 6-2 (p. 65).

These two forms are not of equal status: Younger speakers clearly prefer the forms that are closer to SJ. Nevertheless, you should be able to listen to and understand both forms, even if you cannot freely use both forms.

The commonly used Vernacular Kansai Japanese forms for でき ない are できひん and できへん. Note that the form できへん does not follow the basic pattern. However, it occurs frequently enough that it is worth mentioning. Besides these two, there is one more rather unusual form: でけへん. This form is explained in the next section of this chapter, vowel harmony.

The commonly used Vernacular Kansai Japanese forms for 来られない are 来られへん and 来れへん.

VJ	Group I verb え-form+へん	●●●
VJ	Group I verb ない-form+れへん	●○○
SJ	Group I verb え-form+ない	

VJ	Group II verb ます-form+れへん	●●●
VJ	Group II verb ます-form+られへん	●○○
SJ	Group II verb ます-form+られない	

VJ	できひん, できへん	●●●
VJ	でけへん	●○○
SJ	できない	

VJ	来られへん 来れへん	●●●
SJ	来られない	

EXAMPLE SENTENCES:

① 今日は行かれへん。 I cannot go today.
② 体がついて行けへん。 My body cannot keep up.
③ ゆっくりやろ？耐えれへんわ。 It's so slow. I cannot stand it.
④ タイ料理食べられへん。 I cannot eat Thai food.
⑤ ダンスも全然できひんやろな？ He cannot dance, right?

⑥ ちょっと我慢できへんなっ　　If it becomes so that they cannot
　　たらすぐ離婚とか。　　　　　put up with it, then they'll get
　　　　　　　　　　　　　　　　divorced.

6-8 Vowel harmony

　　When you learned the basic pattern, you may have noticed the importance of the same-sounding vowel. The verbal negative suffix containing the **e** vowel tends to follow stems ending in an **e** vowel, and the verbal negative suffix containing the **i** vowel tends to follow verb stems ending in an **i** vowel. Linguists call this vowel harmony. There is a vowel harmony alternative to the first line of the basic pattern. Recall that the first line reads if **a**, then ～ん. The alternative pattern is as follows. Change the **a** vowel to **e** and then add the ～へん suffix. For example, the vowel harmony negative form of the verb 行く is 行けへん.

　　You have just been introduced to yet another set of overlapping forms. The negative potential form for 行く is 行けない. The VJ variant of this form is 行けへん. But as explained, 行けへん is also the vowel harmony variant for 行かない. As is repeated throughout this book, one characteristic of vernacular language is a large amount of variability in the way to say something (see Section 1-1, p. 9). Another characteristic is that different forms overlap, often resulting in ambiguity (also Section 1-1, p. 9). However, native speakers do not really worry too much about whether the speaker means 'do not' or 'is not able to.' Speakers can always use SJ if the distinction needs to be made clear.

　　Please remember that both the basic pattern and the related vowel harmony pattern are only tendencies; they are not rules. Therefore, speakers often produce forms that do not follow these tendencies. For example, the negative form of 行く is either 行かん (the basic pattern), 行けへん (vowel harmony), or 行かへん (the exceptional form). All three of these forms are used, so you need to be able to understand all three them. Finally, younger speakers tend to interpret the 行(い)けへん vowel harmony as meaning 'not able to go' instead of 'not go,' and so you are recommended to do the same.

> [VJ] Group I verb え-form+へん   ●○○
> [SJ] Group I verb ない-form+ない

EXAMPLE SENTENCES:

① 今(いま)までは、あんまり買(か)えへんかった。 — I haven't bought so much.

② 嫌(きら)いな人(ひと)もおれへん。 — There's no one that bothers me.

③ 旦那(だんな)が分(わ)かれへんと言(い)ってた。 — My husband said that he doesn't understand.

④ 塾(じゅく)とか行(い)けへんかってん。 — I didn't go to cram school, or something like that.

⑤ 東京(とうきょう)の人(ひと)は言(ゆ)えへんよね。 — People from Tokyo don't say that, do they?

⑥ 怪我(けが)してもええからな。死(し)ねへんかったらええねん。 — It is ok if you get hurt. As long as you don't die, then it's fine.

7 More Verbal Patterns

7-1 Positive obligation: 〜なあかん

This pattern is used to tell the listener that something must be done, or that something must happen. In SJ, this form is expressed using expressions such as 〜なければならない and 〜なくてはいけない, with the verb stem inflected for the verbal negative suffix 〜ない. Thus, the SJ form for 'must go' is, for example, 行かなければならい.

The Kansai VJ equivalent of this form is 〜なあかん. Similar to the SJ expression, the verb stem is inflected for the verbal negative suffix 〜ない. Note that this form is closely related to the expression あかん 'to be bad or undesirable.'

This form has a strong regional flavor. In spite of this, speakers clearly prefer it to the SJ equivalent expressions. In fact, even when a speaker is otherwise using SJ to speak, he or she still uses 〜なあかん. This expression is even heard in formal situations, such as workplace meetings. For some reason, the SJ form is avoided. This is most likely because the VJ is a morpheme bundle, and therefore it is much easier to process (as explained in Section 2-4, p. 25).

The positive obligation pattern for the irregular verb する is either せなあかん or しなあかん. The pattern for 来る is 来なあかん. Note that the verb stems in these forms (せ, し, 来) are consistently short vowels. The past tense form of 〜なあかん is 〜なあかんかった.

| VJ | ない-form+なあかん | ••• |
| SJ | ない-form+なければならない, ない-form+なくてはいけない |

EXAMPLE SENTENCES:

① 勉強せなあかんからね。 Because I must study.
② 楽器やらなあかん。 I have to play a musical instrument.

③ 英語で言わなあかんかった。   I had to say it in English.
④ 遠くに行かなあかんかってんな？   Did you have to go far away?
⑤ 仕事はせなあかんからなー。   Well, I have to work.
⑥ 大阪駅まで出てこなあかんの？   Do you have to come out to Osaka station?

7-2 Negative obligation: ～たらあかん

This pattern is used to tell the listener that something must not be done, or something must not happen. The verb stem is inflected for the past tense marker ～た. The SJ equivalent patterns are ～たらだめです and ～てはいけない. The past tense of ～たらあかん is formed by adding ～かった.

VJ	て-form+たらあかん
SJ	て-form+たらだめだ, て-form+てはいけない

EXAMPLE SENTENCES:

① 五十九点やったらあかん。   You must not end up with a grade of 59.
② 絶対したらあかんの？   Must you absolutely not do it?
③ メイクも濃すぎたらあかん。   Your makeup must not be too heavy.
④ ええな思ったらあかんかったな。   You had to not think, "Ok, this is good."

7-3 Permission and advice: ～てええ, ～んでええ

These expressions are used to indicate permission and advice. The form ～てええ is equivalent to the SJ phrase ～てもいい, while the form ～んでええ is equivalent to the SJ phrase ～なくてもいい. Note that も particle tends to be omitted in VJ. Its optionality is indicated below by brackets. Also, the ～ん suffix here is the same verbal negative suffix introduced in Section 6-1 (p. 62). However, the basic pattern introduced in Section 6-1 is not followed here: Speakers seem to consistently use the ～ん variant only, even after the **e** and **i** vowels.

Example sentence ⑥ mixes VJ and SJ. As pointed out in Section 1-2 (p. 13), this subtle mixing happens all of the time, and it is how speakers fine-tune the level of VJ that they are using at any given time.

| VJ | て-form+て(も)ええ, て-form+で(も)ええ | ●●○ |
| SJ | て-form+てもいい | |

| VJ | ない-form+んで(も)ええ | ●●○ |
| SJ | ない-form+なくてもいい | |

EXAMPLE SENTENCES:

① 結婚は遅くてもええかな。　It's ok to get married later.

② 今日は好きにしてええよ。　Today you can do whatever you like.

③ 行かんでもええんちゃうかな。　You don't have to go, right?

④ まだ止めんでええからもうちょっとやろ。　We don't have to stop yet, so let's do (=practice) a bit more.

⑤ そんな喋らんでええやん。　It's just that you don't need to talk that much.

⑥ 高校受験（こうこうじゅけん）せんでいい。　　You don't have to take the high school entrance exam.

7-4　Forms based on 〜て+おく

The forms in this section and the next section are based on the SJ expression 〜ておく, and its inflected forms. The SJ form consists of two morphemes, 〜て and おく. The second part, おく, is derived from the verb 置く, which means to place an object down in a specific position. Historically, this expression meant to prepare some object, and have it on hand for some future event. Here is an example taken from a description of what to do in case of an earthquake:

◇　部屋の中に運動靴を準備しておくと便利です。　　It's convenient to have a pair of running shoes prepared (=on hand) in your room.

Over time, the action of preparation became more and more abstract, and now the SJ expression 〜ておく means to do some activity in advance for some later purpose. The preparation of a physical object is no longer necessary. Here are two examples.

◇　今日はここまでにしておきましょう。　　Let's call it a day. (Let's go as far as here today.)
◇　これを知っておくべきです。　　You should know this.

The first example suggests that stopping at this point is in preparation for making a smooth transition to continuing next time. The second example implies that knowing a certain thing will be useful at some point in the future.

The vernacular form is 〜とく, and inflects as a Group I verb ending in く. This expression for the most part has the same meaning. That is, it often has the feeling of 'to do something in advance.' But in some cases, the expression seems to have completely lost that feeling, and it is not clear that the speaker has some future event in mind at all. In these cases, the expression just means to do something.

As always is the case with suffixes that adjoin to the て-form, verbs stems that are followed by で instead of て (飲んで, 泳いで, etc.) use a slightly different form. In this case, it is どく.

| VJ | て-form+とく, て-form+どく | ••• |
| SJ | て-form+ておく | |

EXAMPLE SENTENCES:

① ここに置いとくわ。　　　I'll leave it here.
② 一つ言っとくけど。　　　I'll tell you one thing.
③ じーっと見とく。　　　　Watch closely.
④ 食べる前にこれ飲んどくね。Drink this before eating, ok?

The conjunctive form, 〜といて, occurs as an alternative to 〜て. In some cases, there is an obvious meaning of doing something in advance. In other cases, there is not such a meaning. Either way, this form is very rare. Instead, 〜といて has taken on a separate grammatical meaning of making a request. This pattern is explained in detail in Section 7-6. Following are some example sentences of 〜といて with conjunctive meaning.

| VJ | て-form+といて, て-form+どいて | ••◦ |
| SJ | て-form+て | |

EXAMPLE SENTENCES:

⑤ そのまま残しといてもいい　I think that you can just leave it as
　 と思うけど。　　　　　　it is.

⑥ 今の能力を持っといて、中学校からもう一回やり直したい。   I want to repeat my education from junior high school, but with the ability that I have now.

⑦ 動画を撮っといて、あとで見るねん。   I'm recording a video so I can watch it later.

The negative form tends to only occur in a specific pattern: 〜とかんと. This is the negative of 〜とく followed by the conditional particle と. This expression means if you do not do something then something will happen. The usual consequence of not doing something is a bad outcome.

VJ	て-form+とかんと, て-form+どかんと ●●○
SJ	て-form+ておかないと

EXAMPLE SENTENCES:

⑧ やっぱり毎日しとかんと硬くなる。   As expected, if you don't do it (=stretch) every day then your body becomes stiff.

⑨ 自分で考えとかんとあかんよ。   You must think about this on your own.

⑩ もう早くしとかんと、な。   If you don't do this soon, then…

VJ	て-form+とけ, て-form+どけ ●●○
VJ	て-form+とき, て-form+どき ●●○
SJ	て-form+ておけ

This is the command form. The SJ command form of おく is おけ, ending in an **e** vowel. The VJ equivalent is おき (see Section 5-3, p. 57). Therefore, there are two different patterns for the command form. Both are used.

EXAMPLE SENTENCES:

⑪ もう少し寝とけ。　　　　　Sleep for a bit longer.
⑫ ちゃんと聞いとけ。　　　　Listen carefully!
⑬ ええ加減にしとけ。　　　　That's enough! (Literally, act in an acceptable manner.)

| VJ | て-form+とけば, て-form+どけば | ●●○ |
| SJ | て-form+ておけば | |

This is the conditional form.

EXAMPLE SENTENCES:

⑭ ピアノやっとけばよかったかなと思って。　　I think it would've been good if I had learned piano (when I was younger).

⑮ 見とけば良かった。　　　It would've been good if (=I wish that) you had seen it.

⑯ やっとけばどう？　　　　How about you do it (in preparation)?

7-5 Request forms ～といて, ～んといて

These forms are used to request the listener to either do or not do something, similar to the SJ expressions ～てください, and ～ないでください.

The forms introduced in this section are derived from the conjunctive form of とく (see the previous section). The conjunctive form of a verb, て-form+て, can be used as an alternative to て-form+て+ください in VJ. Recall that longer expressions tend to shorten. Thus, for example, 食べて can mean 'Please eat it.' Similarly, て

-form+といて can have the same meaning. Recall that one of the characteristics of VJ is that there are often multiple ways to express the same meaning.

The positive forms for the two irregular verbs する and 来る are してといて and 来といて. The negative forms are せんといて and 来んといて respectively.

VJ	て-form+といて	•••
SJ	て-form+てください	

VJ	ない-form+んといて	•••
SJ	ない-form+ないでください	

EXAMPLE SENTENCES:

① ちょっと聞いといて。 Please listen for a bit.
② これ買っといて。 Please buy this.
③ お会計のとこで待っといて。 Please wait at the cash register.
④ もうちょっと遊んどいて。 Play for a bit more.
⑤ 気にせんといて。 Please don't mind.
⑥ そんな笑わんといて。 Please don't laugh that much.
⑦ あまり変なこと言わんといて。 Please don't say stuff that is quite strange.
⑧ 今日雨が降るということ、忘れんといてよ。 Don't forget that it's going to rain today!

7-6 〜よる

This form is used throughout western Japan west of Osaka to indicate that either something is just about to happen, or something is currently happening. This form is not used so much in Osaka and Kyoto.

The English translations use words such as 'almost,' 'just about' and 'just now' in order to capture this feeling. This form inflects as a Group I verb, and its past tense form 〜よった indicates that something almost happened, or at that time, something was in the middle of happening.

SJ does not have a close equivalent expression. Instead, SJ uses the noun ところ to indicate the same grammatical meaning. Following are two examples of SJ.

◇ ちょうど行っているところです。　I'm just now on my way.

◇ もうちょっとで落ちるところでした。　I almost fell down.

| VJ | ます-form+よる |
| SJ | て-form+ているところです, plain form+ところです |

●●○

EXAMPLE SENTENCES:

① 何しよるん。　What are you doing right now?
② おもろい話やったから、バーッと笑いよるわ。　It's an interesting story, and we burst out laughing.
③ 悪いことも言いよるやろうけどな。　I'm saying bad things, aren't I?
④ おばあちゃん見えよる。　I can just now see Grandma!

7-7 ～はる

This form is an auxiliary verb used as an honorific expression. It is the VJ equivalent of the SJ honorific forms, such as お飲みになる 'to drink' and 召し上がる 'to eat.' It is used when talking about an action or activity performed by a person deserving respect. The form is not used when talking about your own actions or activities.

This has a very strong regional flavor to it, and it is not used outside of the Kansai region. Even within the Kansai region, the exact usage of the auxiliary verb varies slightly from location to location. Furthermore, this form is gradually disappearing from the local language. The youngest speakers in the *Corpus of Kansai Vernacular Japanese* use this form much less than the oldest speakers, as illustrated by Figure 7-1.

The form はる is a Group I verb, and inflects the same as other

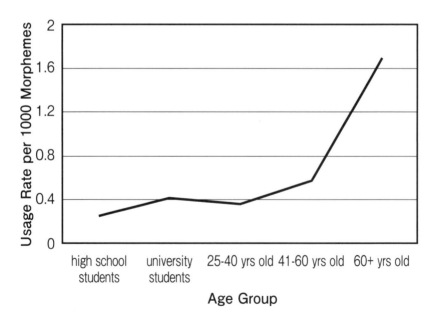

Figure 7-1. The rate of usage of はる per 1000 morphemes.

Group I verbs ending in ある, such as 割る 'to split,' 張る 'to pull taut' and 貼る 'to stick, to paste, to hang up (a poster).'

Similar to other auxiliary verbs, the verb はる follows the main verb. The main verb takes one of three forms. All three forms have the same meaning. As noted in Section 1-1 (p. 9), one of the characteristics of vernacular language is multiple ways of saying the same thing. The three はる forms are as follows.

◇ The main verb may be inflected as the ます-form. In this case, はる directly follows the verb stem in place of 〜ます. Thus, the はる form for 話す is 話しはる.
◇ The main verb may be inflected as for the 〜て suffix. In this case, the 〜て suffix follows the verb stem, and the form はる then follows the 〜て suffix. For example, the はる form for 話す is 話してはる.
◇ The main verb may be inflected as the ない-form. In this case, はる directly follows the verb stem in place of 〜ない. Thus, the はる form for 話す is 話さはる. This inflection pattern is now obsolete, and therefore it may be ignored. The other two forms are worth learning, as they are still used by all generations (just less so by the younger generations).

| VJ | ます-form＋はる | ●●○ |
| SJ | honorific form of the verb | |

EXAMPLE SENTENCES:

① みんな自分の時間を大切にしはる。 — Everyone values their personal time.
② 今でもプリン嫌いな人いはる。 — Even now, there are people who hate pudding.
③ 皆に話しはるんやろ？ — You'll tell everyone, right?
④ 企業行きはる人も多いからね。 — Many people go on to work at a business.

| VJ | て-form+てはる | ●●○ |
| SJ | honorific form of verb+ている | |

EXAMPLE SENTENCES:

⑤ 上手に喋りはるおばあちゃんも居てはると思う。 — I think that there are some grandmothers who speak very well.

⑥ お母さんもお仕事頑張ってはるもんね。えらいね。 — Mother's really diligent about her work, isn't she? It's very noble of her.

⑦ たばこ吸ってはるし、お酒も飲んではるし。 — Because he smokes, and he drinks.

⑧ 似てはるやろ？ — They really look alike, don't they?

The following examples show different inflections for the auxiliary verb はる. These forms are all very rare, but they are easy to understand and remember. These forms may follow either the ます-form (examples ⑫⑬⑭⑮) or the て-form (examples ⑨⑩⑪⑯).

VJ	ます-form+はります/はらへん/はって/はった	●○○
VJ	て-form+はります/はらへん/はって/はった	●○○
SJ	honorific form+ ます/ません/て/た	

EXAMPLE SENTENCES:

⑨ お父さんも言ってはりますけど、仕事楽しいって。 — Father says the same thing, that he enjoys his work.

⑩ 昼からカラオケに行ってはります。 — They go to *karaoke* in the afternoon.

⑪ まだ五歳になってはらへんやろ。 — He's not even five years old yet, right?

⑫ ヨーロッパ行きはらへんよ。 — They won't go to Europe.

⑬ 資格勉強して取りはって。 She studied the requirements, and got qualified.

⑭ 病院まで連れてきてくれはってん。 She brought me to the hospital.

⑮ 前の校長先生が来はった時にも徐々に変えて行きはった。 The previous principal, when he was here, he also gradually changed the system over time.

⑯ お母さんも喜んではったよ。 Mother was also delighted.

8 Sentence-Final Particles

8-1 Overall patterns

This chapter introduces several sentence-final particles that are used differently or are unique to VJ. But before introducing the particles, let us first look at the distribution of sentence-final particles and the ways that they combine with each other.

Table 8-1 lists the ten most frequently used particles and their proportional usage. As can be seen from the table, the particle な is used the most frequently. Therefore, this chapter starts with な. Note that ね, よ, and の are SJ, and therefore they are not covered in this book.

Particle	Proportion
な	36.2%
けど	18.0%
ね	12.5%
ねん	8.1%
よ	5.7%
の	3.7%
わ	3.5%
ん	3.3%
で	3.2%
さ	2.3%
All others	5.8%
Total	100.0%

Table 8-1. The ten most frequent sentence-final particles in VJ.

The particles show interesting co-occurrence patterns with regards to their ability to combine with other sentence-final particles, and the copula forms や, やん, やんか, んや, なんや, and ねんや.

Some of the sentence-final particles are highly restricted in what they may co-occur with while others show much more freedom in this regard. Following is a list of key points concerning the sentence-final particles and these restrictions.

◇   ねん does not have the ability to follow things. It does not follow the other particles, and it does not follow the copula forms んや and なんや (see Section 4-1, p. 39). However, other particles may follow it.
◇   When な combines with other elements, it always follows. It has the ability to follow any of the other forms.
◇   Nothing follows the question marker か except for な.
◇   Next to な, the second most common sentence-final particle is けど. It may follow anything except な and か.

Table 8-2 shows the co-occurrence patterns for ねん, けど, and な. The highlighted forms occur frequently, and are worth mastering.

There is one form missing from the table: ねんけどな. This form occurs somewhat frequently. It occurs after both the copula や and after verbs. It does not occur after んや and its variants, because as mentioned, ねん does not have the ability to follow things.

		Second Component		
		ねん	けど	な
First Component	NP や	やねん	やけど	やな
	NP/VP やん	--	--	やんな
	VP ねん	n/a	ねんけど	ねんな
	VP けど	--	n/a	けどな
	VP か	--	--	かな
	VP ん+や	--	んやけど	んやな
	NP なん+や	--	なんやけど	なんやな
	VP ん+やん	--	--	んやんな

Table 8-2. Co-occurrence restrictions on sentence-final particles. The highlighted forms are very common.

8-2 な

The sentence-final particle な is used in a similar fashion to the SJ sentence-final particle ね. Note that in VJ, this is the default or neutral particle. It is used by both men and women, and by both the younger and older generations. It is not particularly harsh, nor is it particularly rude. But it is also not soft, nor is it polite. Like all of the language introduced in this book, it should really only be used when it is appropriate to use vernacular language. In more formal speech, use ね instead.

This particle is used when you want to add a bit of personal feeling to your statement. It is used to encourage agreement, as in the English expression, '*Don't you think that...*' However, unlike the English, it has much less of a question feeling to it, and the listener does not necessarily feel obliged to answer with a full response.

It can also be used to soften the imperative forms. In such cases, the speaker is commanding the listener, but is adding a slightly softer tone to it, just in case the listener does not agree with the command.

[VJ] Sentence-final particle な •••

EXAMPLE SENTENCES:

① そうやな。 Yeah, that's right.
② よくやるな。 You do it well, don't you?
③ 言われるな。 People say that, don't they?
(Literally, it is said by people.)

The sentence-final particle な is often lengthened to なあ. This is a stronger version of な. It has much more of a '*Don't you think that...*' feeling to it, and listeners feel a stronger obligation to respond, normally in agreement, to the speaker.

| VJ | Sentence-final particle なあ ●●●

EXAMPLE SENTENCES:

④ やりたくなるなあ。　　　　It makes you want to do it, doesn't it?

⑤ 意外とあるなあと思って。　I think there are much more than might be expected.

⑥ 負けてるなあ。　　　　　　I have lost, haven't I?

　　The な particle often occurs together with か as かな. Note that the reverse order never occurs. The combination かな expresses a degree of doubt, and it is a request for confirmation. It feels like the expression '*Wasn't it that…*' used when you cannot remember something exactly and seek confirmation.
　　The combination かな often comes at the end of a small phrase that is only part of a sentence, and it is often in response to a question.

| VJ | Sentence-final particle かな ●●●

EXAMPLE SENTENCES:

⑦ 外で遊ぶかな？　　　　　　We will play outside, won't we?

⑧ 二、三人ちゃうかな？　　　Was it not maybe two, three people?

⑨ 友達の家から、かな？　　　From my friend's house, maybe.

⑩ 小学校三年生ぐらいかな？　About until I was in grade three, I think.

⑪ それぐらいかな？　　　　　About that much, I think.

8-3 ねん

The sentence-final particle ねん has a similar feeling to 〜んや (see Section 4-1, p. 39). It is used to explain something to the listener, such as a reason for doing something. It has a similar feeling to the English phrase '*It is just that...*'

The particle ねん does not combine with 〜んや to produce 〜んやねん. Such a form would contain two parts expressing the same meaning, and therefore ねん would be redundant.

VJ Sentence-final particle ねん

EXAMPLE SENTENCES:

① 好きやねん。 It is just that I like it.
② みんな日本人はそうやねん。 It is just that all Japanese people are like that.
③ とにかく困ることがないねん。 Anyways, there is nothing that I'm troubled by.

ねん often occurs before けど. Adding けど does not change the feeling, and although けど equates to English 'but,' in this case the feeling of contradiction is very weak or non-existent.

VJ Sentence-final particle ねんけど

EXAMPLE SENTENCES:

④ 友達と行ってもいいねんけど。 I could go with a friend.
⑤ 全然何も知らんなと思うねんけど。 It is just that I really think that I don't know anything.

⑥ 月謝とか払ってくれた親に感謝やねんけど。 It is just that I'm really grateful to my parents who pay for the monthly fee (for skating lessons), among other things (such as skates, etc.).

The particle ねん also occurs frequently followed by な. This combines the feelings of explaining something and encouraging agreement.

[VJ] Sentence-final particle ねんな ●●●

EXAMPLE SENTENCES:

⑦ みんな真面目やねんな。 Everyone is so serious, aren't they?
⑧ 決めとけばええのに、決めへんねんな。 It would be great if I decided, but it's just that I cannot decide.
⑨ やっぱりな、退屈やねんな。 As you might expect, it's just that it's boring. (Go figure, it was boring.)

8-4 で

The sentence-final particle で is very close in feeling to the SJ sentence-final particle よ, but its usage is more limited. It tends to only be used to express an assertion with confidence. Unlike よ, it is not used to soften a command, as in the example 行きなさいよ 'Go!' If the command form of the verb is VJ (see Section 5-3, p. 57), then use や instead of よ (see Section 8-6, p. 96, for command forms). In this case, the expression 'Go!' become 行きや.

8 Sentence-Final Particles

[VJ] Sentence-final particle で   ●●●

EXAMPLE SENTENCES:

① そうやで。 That's right!
② ピンはまだおる。だいぶ歳(とし)やで。 I still have my dog, Pin. He's really old!
③ そんな中途半端(ちゅうとはんぱ)なことせえへんで。 I wouldn't do something so halfway like that.
④ めっちゃ旨(うま)い。もう最高(さいこう)やで。 This is really delicious. It is awesome!
⑤ ほとんど遊(あそ)びに行(い)きよるで。 I'm pretty much just going out with my friends.
⑥ 別(べつ)に夢(ゆめ)なんかないで。 I don't have anything like a dream (=goal in life).

The sentence-final particle で may also occur after ねん. This is the only sentence-final particle that co-occurs regularly with で. By adding ねん, the speaker slightly reduces the strength of the assertion.

[VJ] Sentence-final particle ねんで   ●●○

EXAMPLE SENTENCES:

⑦ 携帯一切使(けいたいいっさいつか)わへんねんで。 I never use a cell phone!
⑧ なんか嫌(いや)な臭(にお)いするねんで。 Something smells gross!
⑨ 関空(かんくう)まで行(い)かなあかんねんで。 You have to go all the way to Kansai International Airport!

8-5 わ

The sentence-final particle わ feels like a softer version of the SJ sentence-final particle よ. It has a feeling of the speaker telling the listener something unilaterally. Often, the speaker has decided something and is not really too concerned about whether or not the listener also agrees.

Note that in the Tokyo area, わ tends to be used by women and has a feminine feeling to it. In contrast, in the Kansai area わ is used by both men and women, and so it does not have a feminine feeling to it.

VJ Sentence-final particle わ ●●○

EXAMPLE SENTENCES:

① そんな人見たことないわ。 — I tell you, I have never seen someone like that.

② まぁ、ええわ。 — Ahh, it's fine. (=Forget about it.)

③ そんなの出えへんかったわ。 — They didn't provide something like that.

④ それは分かるわ。 — I also have the same feeling.

⑤ これめっちゃ印象に残ってるわ。 — This really left an impression.

8-6 や

The sentence-final particle や is added onto the end of an utterance to show that the speaker is strongly requesting the listener to do something. It feels similar to the SJ sentence-final particle よ.

This particle looks the same as the VJ copula や, and this may seem confusing. However, the two words are in complementary distribution. In other words, they occur in completely different grammatical patterns. Therefore, the listener can identify whether or not や is a sentence-final particle by the grammatical pattern that it occurs with.

Sentence-final particle や occurs in four patterns, of which one is somewhat unusual. The three usual patterns are all used to request the listener to do something. They are the command form, the volitional form, and the verbal suffix 〜て. The unusual pattern is the morpheme bundle いい+や. Each of these forms is introduced in turn.

The verbal command forms were introduced in Section 5-3 (p. 57). The verbal command forms are used to demand or strongly request that the speaker did something. Adding や onto the end slightly softens the strength of the request. Nevertheless, such forms should not be used with people who are your superiors.

The verbal volition forms end in 〜おう, as in 行こう and 食べよう. Again, adding や slightly softens the tone.

The form 〜て is an abbreviation of 〜てください. The ください ending is dropped in VJ (recall that VJ is often just a shortened form of polite SJ), and adding や makes it clear that the speaker's intention is a request.

[VJ] Sentence-final particle や   ●●○

EXAMPLE SENTENCES:

① お姉さん、なんかしいや。   Sister, do something!
② 洗濯物ちゃんと出しや。   Put out the laundry!
③ 一回日本食作ろうや。   Let's make Japanese food at least once!
④ ハワイ行こうや。   Let's go to Hawaii!

⑤ もうちょっと考えてや。　　Think about this a bit more, will you?

⑥ 教えてや。　　Tell me (the secret)!

 This leaves the one usual usage of や. This sentence final-final particle is sometimes used after the い-adjective いい, and its VJ variant, ええ. It has a feeling of assertively telling the listener that it is fine, or that there is no problem. It can be used in response to the question, '*Why did you do that?*' when the person asking is implying that doing so may not have been a very wise thing to do. By responding いいや, the responder reassures that there is no problem, and that an explanation is not needed.

 It can be used with the adverb もう to indicate that the responder feels that it is enough. Note that the expression いいや is a morpheme bundle, and therefore it always occurs in that form. For example, the past tense form よかったや is not possible.

VJ　いいや, ええや　　　　　　　　　　　●○○

EXAMPLE SENTENCES:

⑦ じゃあもういいや。話変えよう。　　Then that's enough; let's change the topic.

⑧ 失敗してもいいやと思ってさ。　　Because I think it's fine if I fail.

⑨ もうええや、飽きたと思うんやけど。　　It is just that to me that is enough, as I feel that I am fed up with it.

8-7 っけ

This sentence-final particle is an abbreviation of the word だけ 'just, only.' Its usage shows that the speaker is trying to remember something, and is asking the listener for confirmation about the forgotten memory. An example of the word だけ used in this manner is the phrase 何だっけ 'just what (was it).' The VJ variant of this phrase is given as example sentence ②.

VJ っけ ●○○

EXAMPLE SENTENCES:

① 彩香もアメリカやったっけ？   Didn't Ayaka also go to the United States?
② なんやっけ？   What was it again?
③ 部活やってたっけ？   Didn't you do some club activity?
④ 見せたっけ？   Did I show this to you already?

8-8 さ

The last sentence-final particle introduced is さ. It is often pronounced with a long vowel as さー. This particle occurs not only at the end of sentences but also in the middle of them. This particle is used by the speaker as 相槌. This term refers to Japanese speakers periodically requesting the listener to acknowledge that they are listening and understand. In other words, the meaning of this sentence-final particle is 'Are you listening?' English speakers use expressions such as 'yeah, yeah,' 'uhuh' and 'go on' to express the same feeling of understanding. However, 相槌 is used much more frequently in conversational Japanese than in English.

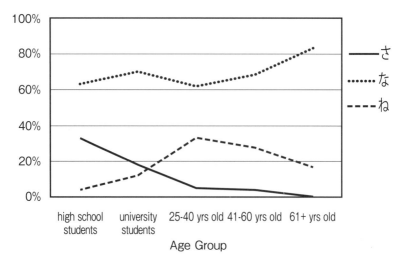

Figure 8-1. The use of three aizuchi particles by age group.

The SJ 相槌(あいづち) form used by the speaker is ね. When speaking SJ, the listener normally responds to ね with はい. When speaking VJ, the response to 相槌(あいづち) is a short ん sound, or even just nodding the head.

Traditionally, the VJ 相槌(あいづち) form used by the speaker was な. All three of these particles さ, ね and な occur at the end of the sentence as sentence-final particles and in the middle of the sentence as 相槌(あいづち). The VJ variant is gradually shifting to さ. Figure 8-1 shows the proportional rates of usage for さ, な, and ね when used in the middle of sentences. As can be seen in the figure, さ is slowly gaining popularity among the younger generations. The use of さ is particularly favored by young men. If you are younger than 25 years old (and you want to sound young), then you should be using さ in your VJ. Older speakers are fine using only な. Of course, in formal situations, you should use ね regardless of age.

Let us take a look a young male speaker who uses さ frequently. The following is a short excerpt from his conversational interview in the *Corpus of Kansai Japanese*. He is explaining that he would like to visit Korea and go to a club. Apparently, this young man mistakenly believes that they only let beautiful people into dance clubs in Korea. He has just commented that it must be tough to be a father in Korea. Note that the following example is said as one sentence (see Section 2-2, p. 20 for an explanation of why), and that during this sentence he uses さ six times. From this short example, you can get a feeling for how much 相槌 is used in conversation, and just how frequently young men use さ these days.

例えばよ、娘がさ、今日もクラブ行ってくるわって言ってさ、	For example, your daughter, is like "I'm goin' to a club,"
「クラブ、そんなん行くなー」って怒ってさ、	and you're like, "Stop goin' to clubs so much!" all angry like,
「うるせえんだよ」って感じで、バッて出てってさ、	and then she's like, "Shut up!" or somethin' and rushes off to the club,
「不細工です」って止められて、	but she's stopped from going in and told, "You're ugly!"
帰ってきたらお父さんさ、	so she comes home early, and her father,
「お前なにしに帰ってきたんや」って言ってさ、	he's like, "What did you come home for?"
「不細工だから止められたよ」ってさ、	and she says, "I was stopped because I'm ugly,"
「ごめん」って絶対気まずいと思うねん、俺は。	"Ah man, I'm sorry to hear that!" I would feel crappy.

VJ さ, さー ●●●

EXAMPLE SENTENCES:

① 始まる時さー、ドキドキしない？ — Don't you get excited when (the concert) starts?

② めっちゃ喧嘩するしさ。 — Well, because they fight a lot.

③ 部屋を片付けたりさ、勉強したりさ。 — I do things like clean up my room and study.

9 って

9-1 Background

Although って is technically just another particle, it is used frequently in VJ, and in different ways. Therefore, って gets its own chapter. This particle is a shortened version of several different SJ particles and phrases. The SJ equivalent expression depends on the exact usage.

This particle is most often pronounced as って, with a geminate t sound (two t sounds in a row, as indicated by the small っ). However, geminate sounds only occur after vowels. After the consonantal sound ん, って is pronounced as just て. Furthermore, って is sometimes reduced to just て even after a vowel. Recall that two of the characteristics of vernacular language are multiple variants for the same form, and that forms tend to shorten.

9-2 As a vernacular variant of と

One of the most frequent usages of って is as a vernacular variant of the SJ particle と when used with verbs such as 言う and 思う.

> VJ って+verbs such as 言う, 思う, etc.　•••
> SJ 〜と+verbs such as 言う, 思う, etc.

103

EXAMPLE SENTENCES:

① 男いるって言っても先生ぐらいやんか。 — Even though I said that there are men, it's just that they are all pretty much just teachers.

② 看護士はきついって言うけど。 — They say that nursing is really tough.

③ 「しなくていいよ」って言われたら喜ぶ？ — Would you be happy if you were told that you didn't have to do it?

④ 怖いって思って、めっちゃ。 — I felt scared, really scared.

⑤ 違うなって思う？ — Do you think that it's different?

9-3 Report the contents of a request, decision, etc.

The particle って is used to report the contents of a request, decision, feeling, understanding, fact, etc. It is also used to report the name of a person, place, or thing. Unlike the SJ particle と, って can occur directly before a noun phrase such as こと or 人. In this case the SJ equivalent phrase is という.

| VJ | って+NP |
| SJ | ～という |

| VJ | って+VP |
| SJ | ～と |

EXAMPLE SENTENCES:

① もうええかって感じかな？ — It was a feeling of already having had enough, wasn't it?

② 料理を勉強したってこと？ — So it's that you have learned cooking?

③ マイケル・バイカートって人が、作った曲やねん。   It is a song written by someone called Michael Weikath.

④ あたしが英語ぺらぺらじゃないって分かっている。   She understands that I'm not fluent in English.

⑤ もう大学は介護にしようって決めたから。   Because I decided to take nursing at university.

⑥ 作ってくれって頼まれる研究所があるやんな。   It is just that there is a research center that was requested to make it.

9-4 Repeat what was said

Another frequent usage of って is to repeat what another person has said. Either the exact words, or just the main contents of the message, are repeated followed by って at the end of the utterance.

VJ って
SJ 〜と言った，〜だそうだ

EXAMPLE SENTENCES:

① 行きたい、って。   She said, "I want to go."

② 大丈夫や、大丈夫や、って。   And he was like, "I'm ok, I'm ok."

③ 知らん子やったけど、「ありがとうございます」って。   I didn't know her, but she was like, "Thank you very much!"

④ 頼むから黙れ、って。   And he goes, "I'm asking you to shut up!"

⑤ 何々家の結婚式にご参加ですか、って。   And the man (at the reception desk) said, "Which family's wedding ceremony will you be participating in today?"

9-5 Indicate the topic

The particle is used to indicate the topic of the sentence. Often this is done in order to explain or further clarify the topic. The form ってば is also used in this manner as an alternative to just って. It is a shortened form of と言えば.

| VJ | って, ってば | ●●○ |
| SJ | 〜というのは, 〜と言えば |

EXAMPLE SENTENCES:

① 具体的な違いって何やろ？ What is the concrete (=specific) difference between them?

② 今から二十年後の自分って何してると思う？ What do you think you will be doing twenty years from now?

③ 意外に優しいよな、人間って。 Humans are kinder than one might expect, aren't they?

④ ゴキブリってば大敵よな。 Cockroaches are our number one enemy, aren't they?

⑤ やっぱりイタリアって、多いん？ Are there many in Italy then, as one might expect?

9-6 Clarify something

The particle って is used to clarify the meaning of something. It has a feeling of '*When you say..., do you mean...*' The form ってば may also be used is this way.

| VJ | って, ってば | ●●○ |
| SJ | 〜というのは, 〜と言えば |

EXAMPLE SENTENCES:

① ネパールってヒマラヤ山脈のところですよね？ — Nepal, that is the Himalayan Mountains, isn't it?

② 昔っていつ？ — When you say "the past," when do you mean?

③ サイロって何？ — What do you mean by "silo"?

④ 洗礼って水のやつやったっけ？ — Baptism...Is that the one with water?

⑤ 「手ぬぐい」って、小さいタオル？ — A *te'nugui*, is that a small towel?

9-7 Emphasize that you already said something

This particle is also used to repeat with emphasis something that you have already said to the listener. The speaker is telling the listener to stop ignoring what he or she has already said. The form ってば may also be used in this way.

VJ	って, ってば
SJ	～と言ったでしょう

EXAMPLE SENTENCES:

① 分かってるよ、もう言うな、って！ — I know! I told you to stop telling me that.

② そんなこと知ってる、って！ — I told you, I know that.

③ テーブルを揺らすな、って！ — I told you to stop shaking the table. Now stop!

④ もういい、ってば！ — I told you enough already!

9-8 だって

The particle って combines with the SJ copula だ to form だって. This expression is used at the start of an utterance, and connects the following utterance with something that was just said. It indicates that the following utterance is a clarification of what was just said. The clarification is either a reason for the previous utterance, or further explanation of the previous utterance.

When the preceding utterance was also spoken by different speaker, then the expression だって often suggests a feeling of disagreement. In this case, だって introduces the reason for disagreeing.

> [VJ] だって
> [SJ] なぜかというと (same person speaking)
> [SJ] それでも, だとしても (different people speaking)

EXAMPLE SENTENCES (SAME PERSON):

① 方言は面白いよね。だって単語単語で違う。
Dialect is interesting. I mean, every word is different.

② めっちゃドラマ見てる。だって、全百六十何話とかやもん。
I'm watching tons of drama shows. I mean, some of them have over 160 episodes.

③ 全然違うな。だって、たまに通じひん時あるよ。
The language is totally different. I mean, there are even times when I cannot understand.

④ おばちゃんは、ため口。だって絶対年下やねん。
I speak non-polite language with your aunt. After all, she's younger than me.

EXAMPLE SENTENCES (DIFFERENT PEOPLE):

⑤ A. どこ行きたい？
B. フランスの田舎の方とか。
A. なんで？
B. えっ、なんで？
A. だって都会の方が楽しそうじゃない？

A. Where do you want to go?
B. The countryside of France.
A. Why?
B. What? Why?
A. I mean, doesn't a big city seem more enjoyable?

⑥ A. あ、全然敬語ちゃうくていい。
B. だって緊張する。

A. Oh, it's ok to not use honorific language.
B. Yes, but I'm nervous.

⑦ A. 何歳でお姉ちゃんを産んだんやったっけな？
B. お姉ちゃんが二十三歳の終わり。
A. まじで。すぐやん。
B. だって一月に結婚して、十二月にできてるから。別に早くないよ。

A. At what age was it that you gave birth to older sister?
B. Older sister was at the end of age 23.
A. Seriously? That was soon.
B. You say that, but I got married in January, and then got pregnant in December. That is not so quick.

9-9 ってゆうか

This expression is composed of the VJ quotative marker って, the verb 言う, and the question marker か. The expression literally means 'Do you say...?' The VJ question patterns described in Section 4-4 (p. 42) are often used instead of the question marker か. As a reminder, they are の, ん, and using a rising intonation.

Following are examples.

| VJ | ってゆう+か/の/ん/rising intonation ●●○
| SJ | 〜と言いますか

EXAMPLE SENTENCES:

① 今やったら何ってゆうの？   What do you call it these days?
② 接着剤ってゆうか？あれ。   Is that "adhesive" (= strong glue)?
　 分かれへん。   I'm not sure.
③ 胴囲のところの、胴囲って   The circumference of the waist…
　 ゆうん？ここ。   Do you call this area here the
　 circumference of the waist?

　　A much more common usage of ってゆうか is when the speaker wants to rephrase something immediately said. It has a feeling of 'Well, I just said A, but rather than A, it is more like B.' Note that SJ does not have a corresponding equivalent phrase. A shorter alternative to ってゆうか is ってか.

| VJ | ってゆうか, ってか ●●○

EXAMPLE SENTENCES:

④ 日本の映画そんな好きじゃ   I don't really like Japanese movies
　 ないってゆうか、洋画しか観 that much, or rather, I only watch
　 いひん。   western movies.
⑤ インタビューってゆうか、普 It was more like a normal
　 通の会話だったんですけど。 conversation than an interview.
⑥ スキー、ってかスノボに行   I go skiing, or rather snowboarding.
　 ったりする。
⑦ やったことはあるよ、って   Yeah, I have done that, or rather, I
　 ゆうか、今やってる。   should say, I'm doing it now.

Another commonly occurring pattern is the combination of な
ん with ってゆう followed by a question maker such as か or の.
Note that when って follows the consonantal sound ん, it reduces to
て. Thus, this combination when followed by か becomes なんてゆう
か. This means 'What do you say?' and is used when the speaker is
trying to recall the way of saying something, or deciding on the best
expression to use.

| VJ | なんてゆう+か/の/ん/rising intonation ••• |
| SJ | 何と言いますか |

EXAMPLE SENTENCES:

⑧ 自分が、なんてゆうか、その仕事合ってるとか、そうゆうことも重要やと思う。

I feel that, what do you say? Does the job fit? That is important.

⑨ 真理子ちゃんはね、なんてゆうか、活発な子やったね。

Mariko was, how should I say, an active child.

⑩ 小さい時よく、なんてゆうか、秘密基地、作ったりした。

When I was small, I often made, what do you call it? Secret forts.

⑪ ちょっとフワっとした。なんてゆうかな、キッとした感じより、フワーって感じ。

It was soft. What do you say? It was much more of a soft feeling than a sharp feeling.

⑫ ほか、なんて言うか学生時代、高校時代に放課後とかどうゆう活動してた？

Other than that, during your, what do you call it, student days, or rather high school days, what activities did you do after school?

10 Expressions of Vagueness

10-1 Background

This chapter introduces several expressions of vagueness. These expressions are used frequently in VJ in roughly two different situations.

The first situation is when the speaker is not able to be precise. This may be because the speaker has forgotten the details, or perhaps did not know the details in the first place.

The second situation is when the speaker wants to soften his or her words in order to reduce the sharpness of the tone. This is useful in situations such as disagreeing with someone, criticizing something or talking about a sensitive topic.

10-2 みたいな

The first expression is みたいな. This expression is historically derived from the expression 見た+よう, which means 'to look like.' Over time, the two parts merged and were shortened to みたい. Nowadays, the expression means 'it seems to be… or something like that.'

According to SJ grammar books, the word みたい inflects as a な-adjective. な-adjectives are followed by な when they modify a following noun, as in 綺麗な人 'a pretty person' and 大変なこと 'a horrible thing.' When used in this way, the word みたい indicates that the following noun resembles the phrase that comes before it.

| VJ | NP/VP みたいなNP | ••• |
| SJ | NP のようなNP, NP/VP みたいなNP |

EXAMPLE SENTENCES:

① スイスみたいな国じゃないけども。
But it's not a country like Switzerland.

② スポーツ関係に就職したいみたいなことは聞いたけどな。
So I heard that you want to work for a sports-related company, or something like that.

③ 最後、天丼屋さんみたいなとこ行きましたよ。
In the end, we went to place like a *tendon* restaurant.

④ サークルみたいなもんやけどな。
It is something like a university club.

⑤ もう一人のお嬢さんみたいな子は、銀行マンと結婚した。
And the other girl, the one like a princess, married a bank employee.

In formal SJ, な-adjectives are followed by the copula です when used as the predicate of the sentence, as in the sentence あの人は綺麗です 'That person is pretty.' The word みたい may also be used in this way, as shown by the following examples:

◇ 違うみたいですね。 It seems that this is wrong.
◇ 韓国語喋れるみたいです。 It seems that he can speak Korean.

The VJ equivalent of みたいです is just みたい. However, the word みたい is used so often as the form みたい+な (the form that occurs before a noun) that the two parts have literally fused together as a morpheme bundle to form a single word, and these days speakers almost never use みたい alone: It is almost always followed by な. Note that this な is not the sentence-final particle な. In fact, the sentence-final particle な can be added on to the end of みたいな to form みたいなな, as seen in example ⑦.

VJ	NP/VPみたいな
SJ	ます-form+そうです, NP/VPらしいです

EXAMPLE SENTENCES:

⑥ もうしゃあない、みたいな。   And then he was like, "It cannot be helped," or something like that.

⑦ 教えてくれたみたいなな。   It seems that they just told us, right?

⑧ ちょっと無理かな、みたいな？   It seems a bit hopeless, right?

⑨ 勉強ちょっとする、みたいなさ。   She goes, "I'll study for a bit," or something like that.

⑩ 俺も嫌いっすわ、みたいなこと言われた。   I was told "I hate it too," or something like that.

10-3 感じ

The word 感じ means 'feeling,' and it is the nominal form of the verb 感じる 'to feel.' The word 感じ is used at the end of the utterance to add vagueness. Although it originally meant 'a feeling of,' its meaning has now expanded to mean 'It seems to be… or something like that.' In other words, it has the same feeling as the expression みたいな, and the two may be combined together as みたいな感じ without any change in meaning.

Of course, the word 感じ still retains the meaning of 'feeling' and is used to refer to the sense of touch. Similar to the English word 'feeling,' the word 感じ is also used more abstractly to mean 'impression,' 'characteristic,' or 'atmosphere.'

Note that the 感じ is a noun, and therefore it should be followed by a copula. However, in VJ the copula after a noun may be deleted. This is particularly so after the word 感じ. (Recall that frequently occurring forms often shorten.)

VJ	～感じ	•••
SJ	～という印象 'impression,' という雰囲気 'atmosphere'	

VJ	～感じ	•••
SJ	ます-form+そうです, NP/VP らしいです	

EXAMPLE SENTENCES:

① そういう感じやね。　　　　　Yeah, it's like you said.

② お兄ちゃんもそんな感じやった？　Was your older brother also like that?

③ カフェみたいな感じ？　　　　An atmosphere like a coffee shop?

④ 結構自由に遊べる感じ。　　　It was like I pretty much was able to play whenever I wanted to.

⑤ いつ休みやねん、みたいな感じや。　I'm like, "So when do I get a day off?"

⑥ これでええやろう、みたいな感じで言った。　He said it with a tone that was like "So this is good enough, right?"

10-4 なんか

This expression has its roots in the word 何か 'something.' In VJ, it is pronounced as なんか. It has several different usages. These are introduced in turn.

The first usage is the combination of question marker か+なんか. This combination follows noun, and indicates that noun, or something like that noun.

VJ	NP かなんか	•••
SJ	NP かなにか	

EXAMPLE SENTENCES:

① いや、韓国じゃないかな。台湾かなんか。 — No, it wasn't Korea, was it? It was Taiwan, or somewhere like that.

② 最初に売り切れた物が焼きそばかなんかやった。 — The first thing sold out was *yakisoba*, or something like that.

③ そこに、なんか石かなんか知らんけど、隠してあるんやけど。 — There was, I don't know, a rock or something like that, hidden there.

④ 部活空手部かなんかしとったやんな。 — You were in the *karate* club, or something like it, right?

⑤ そうか。お姉ちゃんかなんかいるねんな？ — Oh, that's right. You have an older sister, or something like that, right?

The question marker か can be replaced with the particle とか. This has the same meaning as 〜かなんか.

| VJ | NP とかなんか |
| SJ | NP とかなにか |

EXAMPLE SENTENCES:

⑥ 象のキーホルダーとかなんか売ってた。 — They sold things like elephant key chains.

⑦ おもろいエピソードみたいなとかなんかある？ — Do you have some interesting episodes (=stories), or something like that (from your trip)?

⑧ 大雨警報とかなんか多くない？ — Are there many heavy rain warnings, and things like that?

⑨ 思い出とかなんかないですか？ — Do you not have any good memories, or something like that (from that time)?

⑩ 地元の特産品とかなんか思いつくものある？ — Are there any local specialty goods that you can think of?

The phrases かなんか and とかなんか are also used after verbal phrases. In this case, it means 'to do… or something like that.'

> VJ VP かなんか, VP とかなんか　　　●●○
> SJ VP かなにか, VP とかなにか

EXAMPLE SENTENCES:

⑪ なんか迎え、親が忘れとったかなんかで、電話してんけど。 — The parent forgot to come get her kid, or something like that, so I called her.

⑫ あんたら二人結婚するとかなんか言ってるけど。 — Well, you two say that you are going to get married, or something like that.

⑬ 今後もう一回行ってみたいとかなんか、そう言う場所あるんですか？ — Is there anywhere that you want to go to one more time, or somewhere like that?

⑭ あなたのお子様の就職を考えるかなんかって言う。 — And so he says, "Are you thinking about your child's employment," or something like that.

⑮ その時に遅いのかなんか知らんけど。 — Well, I don't know if it will be like too late by then.

The word is used near the beginning of an utterance to soften it, and add room for doubt. It adds a general feeling of 'something like…' There is not an equivalent SJ expression that could be used in formal situations.

| VJ | NP なんか used as a softener word　●●●

EXAMPLE SENTENCES:

⑯ 今までなんか、人間関係で、あかんな、みたいなんとかもあったの？　　Have there been times, like, in your relations with others, which were like horrible?

⑰ ちょっと周りが、なんか言い過ぎ？　　The people around him maybe said too much, don't you think?

⑱ 映画館に行くことはないな。なんか、借りて観るタイプやから。　　I never go to the movie theater. I'm more the type to borrow and watch a movie at home.

The word なんか is used as filler, similar to English 'ummm...' This indicates that the speaker is trying to think of what to say. This usage is similar to the SJ filler words あの and えっと.

| VJ | NP なんか used as a filler word　●●●
| SJ | あの, えっと

EXAMPLE SENTENCES:

⑲ あのー、なんか、あのー、ちょっとまー。　　Ummm, well, hmmm, ahhh, yeah.

⑳ それで終わりっていう、そう言う、なんか、何、そう言う態度やったんやけど。　　It was just that he had this, like what do you call it, like attitude that it was like over.

㉑ えっと、なんか今、今これは無理みたいなんや、って。　　And she was like, "Ummm, well, right now, right now is not possible."

Finally, among younger speakers, the word なんか is used with a feeling of 相槌, similar to the sentence-final particle さ introduced in Section 8-6 (p. 96). In this case, なんか has very little meaning at all, and it is just an empty filler word. This usage is similar to the one just introduced, which has feeling similar to English 'ummm,' in that the word has no real meaning. When used this way, the word has a feeling similar to the English filler word 'like.' This usage is most popular among young women. The following speech example, taken from the *Corpus of Kansai Vernacular Japanese*, consists of two female university students talking about the Kansai dialect. One of them is telling a story about how the girl that she was working with at a part-time job did not understand the VJ expression 帰りよる. (The grammar point verb stem+よる is explained in Section 7-6, p. 83.)

The word なんか has been highlighted. Observe how frequently the two of them use なんか as they converse. Their usage rate is about once per every fifteen seconds. This is an extreme example chosen to illustrate a point; nevertheless, なんか is used very frequently, particularly by younger women.

A. 普通になんか、普通の関西弁やと思ってたのに通じひんとか。

A. I like, every day, I thought I was using every day Kansai dialect, but it was not understood.

B. 何が、なんか例えばなんか覚えてる？

B. What, for example? Is there like something you can remember?

A. なんか、あのよくあの、スタッフのなんか、のれんくぐった向こう側でさあ、

そこで、なんか中で作業してて外ががやがやし始めたから。

あ、お客さんもう帰りよって？ってその同じバイトの子に聞いたら、

A. Like, well, often, well, the staff's, through the little curtain (that leads to the kitchen area), on the other side,
back there, I was like working, and I heard some noises start on the other side of the curtain.

So I was like, "The customers are about to go home now?" to the other girl working with me.

え？って言われて、なんか、えっ、どう言うこと？って言われた。

And she was like, "What? What does that mean?"

10-5 ～的

The suffix ～的 is added onto a noun to form a な-adjective. For example, 的 is added on to noun 基本 'base' to form the adjective 基本的 'basic.' The particle に can then be added on to form an adverb as in 基本的に 'basically.' The Japanese suffix ～的 is highly productive. This means that 的 can be added on to new nouns as they come into the language, and it can be added onto any noun that is already in use. The closest English equivalent to this is the suffix -*ish*, which can also be attached to any noun.

When ～的 is used in this manner, it has a feeling of 'something that is like.' In other words, this is an alternative to ～みたいな. However, ～的 is used with much less frequency.

[VJ] NP 的な ●●○
[SJ] NP のような

EXAMPLE SENTENCES:

① 日本人的な働き方ではないからな。

Well, they don't have a Japanese-ish work style.

② ちょっとアルバイト的なこともやったな。

I also did a bit of part-time work-ish type stuff.

③ 生ゴミね、生ゴミ的なものやったら畑に撒いたり、あのー、してたやん。

I took the raw garbage, if it was raw garbage-like stuff then I spread it around on the fields.

④ 友達が転校するからさよな　　Our friend was transferring to a
らパーティ的なことしよう　　new school, so he told everyone,
よ、みたいな話やってんな。　"Let's do something party-ish" or
something like that.

There is a special use of 的 that needs to be pointed out. When used after a pronoun such as 私 or a noun indicating an individual such as お母さん, it means 'In my / his / her own way.' It implies that the individual is different from others, and has a unique and personal way of doing things.

| VJ | pronoun or noun indicating person+的に ●○○
| SJ | pronoun or noun indicating person+なりに

EXAMPLE SENTENCES:

⑤ 私的にあかんなって思うけ　　In my own way, I think it's not
ど。　　　　　　　　　　　　good.
⑥ 俺的に考えるのが、最近の　My own way of thinking is that
女性めっちゃ強いやんか。　these days women are quite strong.
⑦ めっちゃ我慢したなって感　In my own way, I really feel like I
じやわ、俺的には。　　　　did a good job of putting up with it.
⑧ そやけども、お母さん的に　Well, yes but in your mom's own
は嬉しいって言ったことは　way, she has said that she's happy.
ありますね。
⑨ でも若い、なんか韓国の妹　But she's young, and her existence
的な存在。　　　　　　　　is like "Korea's little sister."

Finally, in VJ the Japanese suffix 〜的 may also follow a VP or even a full clause. Again, it means the same as 〜みたいな.

| VJ | VP 的　　　　　　　　　　　　　　　　　　●○○
| SJ | VP そうです, VP らしいです

122

EXAMPLE SENTENCES:

⑩ パパが仕事でアメリカ行ってて、で、五年ぐらいパパとママがアメリカ住んでて、うちが生まれちゃった的な。

Daddy went to the States for work, and mommy and daddy lived there for five years, and then it seems that I was born.

⑪ ちょっと遊ぼうよ的なことになってな。

It became so that it was like, "Let's get together."

⑫ 新作入ってきましたよ的な、お声かけしたりした。

I called out to people as they went by, something like "I have new product!"

⑬ まあカレー頼んだ時点で、ナンも頼まなあかん的なオーラ出すから。

When the customer ordered curry, then at that point I gave off an aura that was something like, "You've got to order nan bread too!"

⑭ A. え、がばしょって何？
B. 知らん。頑張りましょう的なことちゃうん？

A. What is *gabasho*?
B. I don't know. Isn't it something like *ganbarimashō* (='to do your best')?

10-6 〜ら, 〜らへん

In SJ, the plural marker 〜たち can be added onto a noun to form the plural. This is most often used with pronouns. Thus, the plural forms of the first and second person pronouns 私 and あなた are 私たち and あなたたち. There are other plural markers besides 〜たち, including the plural marker 〜ら. Compared to 〜たち, 〜ら has a much more vernacular feeling to it. The following are some examples of the use of 〜ら as a plural marker with a pronoun.

| VJ | NP ら |
| SJ | NP たち |

EXAMPLE SENTENCES:

① 「あんたら二人(ふたり)で行(い)って来(き)い」って。 — He was like, "You two go alone!"

② 僕(ぼく)らの時代(じだい)は、冬(ふゆ)はスキーに行(い)くって言(い)うのが当(あ)たり前(まえ)やった。 — In our time (=when I was a student), going skiing in the winter was the obvious thing to do.

③ うちら女(おんな)の子(こ)ばっかりや。 — We are all girls.

④ あたしら全員(ぜんいん)が好(す)きやからなあ。 — Because we all like it.

The plural marker 〜ら is also used with pronouns even when the speaker does not necessarily intend to pluralize the pronoun. This adds a sense of vagueness to the sentence, as if the speaker is talking about people in general. Thus, 私ら has a feeling of 'someone such as myself.' Following are examples of 〜ら used in this manner. Note that there is not a corresponding SJ equivalent expression.

[V.J] NP ら   ●●○

EXAMPLE SENTENCES:

⑤ あんたら大学(だいがく)出(で)たけど、ほんまに就職(しゅうしょく)あるんかな。 — You have graduated from university, but can a person like you really get a job?

⑥ 僕(ぼく)、僕(ぼく)らは基本的(きほんてき)にそんなにむちゃくちゃ賭(か)けたりせえへん。 — I, people like me basically don't gamble such a crazy amount.

⑦ お父(とう)さんらよりずっと若(わか)い人(ひと)やったみたいやな。 — It seems like it was someone much younger than someone like me (your father).

⑧ うちらは覚(おぼ)えてへんけど。 — I don't remember that.

The suffix 〜ら may also be combined with the suffix 〜へん to form the compound suffix 〜らへん. The suffix 〜へん is derived from the noun 辺, which means 'neighborhood' or 'vicinity,' as in the expression この辺 'this vicinity' or 'roughly here.' The compound suffix 〜らへん is used to indicate an approximate location or an approximate point in time. Following are several example sentences illustrating this usage.

VJ NP+らへん　　　　　　　　　　　　　　　●●○
SJ NP の辺り, NP ごろ

EXAMPLE SENTENCES:

⑨ そこらへん外国人の観光客多いって聞いてる。
I heard that there are lots of foreigner tourists in that area.

⑩ だいたいどこらへんに行ってたんですか？
Whereabouts did you go?

⑪ 神戸のどこらへんですか？
Whereabouts in Kobe?

⑫ 上野さんが住んでるとこらへんやん？
Is that about where Ms. Ueno is living?

⑬ 最初らへんだけ。
Just around the beginning only.

⑭ 二回生の時らへんに先輩から告白されたやんか。
About when I was a second year university student, my *senpai* confessed that she liked me.

11 The Special Status of 「ん」

11-1 Sentence-final particle ん

This chapter introduces several cases in which the particle の may optionally be pronounced as ん. Such a variant is a strong marker of VJ, and should only be used in a casual context.

The first case is the sentence-final particle の, which was introduced in Section 4-4 (p. 42) as a question marker. In VJ, the sentence-final の may optionally be realized as ん. Speakers of all ages and both genders use the の and ん variants at roughly the same rate when speaking VJ.

| VJ | Sentence-final particle の→ん | ••• |
| SJ | Sentence-final particle か |

EXAMPLE SENTENCES:

① 親は何も言ってないん？　Did your parents not say anything?
② お母さんは髪どうしてたん？　What happened to your mother's hair?
③ 何がいいん？　What is good about it?
④ 大阪じゃないん？　Isn't it Osaka?
⑤ いつからその夢持っとったん？　From when did you have such a dream?
⑥ 毎日何時に寝てるん？　What time do you sleep every day?
⑦ 何なん？　What is it? (なの→なん, see Ch. 4-4)

11-2 NP ん NP

The particle の is also used in SJ to indicate a genitive relationship between two nouns. This is shown in English by either *'s* or the word *of*, as in the examples *Tom's book*, or *the flag of Canada*. The SJ genitive particle の may reduce to ん in VJ. However, speakers seem to only do this in very-frequently occurring morpheme bundles. Even then, the actual usage of ん instead of の is still very rare. In fact, 95% of the examples of ん found in the *Corpus of Kansai Vernacular Japanese* occur before one of four words: 時, ところ (or its variant とこ), 中, and ち. The last one, ち, is the abbreviated form of 家, and means 'my place.'

The pattern of の reducing to ん is used so rarely that there is little value in learning it. However, considering that it is just one more example of の reducing to ん—the main theme of this chapter—then it is also almost effortless to learn. Certainly being able to listen to and comprehend the four common patterns will help increase your overall listening comprehension of VJ. The following are examples of these common patterns.

| VJ | ～ん時, ～んところ・とこ, ～ん中, ～んち | ●○○ |
| SJ | ～の時, ～のところ, ～の中, ～の家 | |

EXAMPLE SENTENCES:

① 高校ん時に俺ずっと遊んでた。 — When I was a high school student, I goofed off all the time.

② 中一ん時、田中先生やったっけ？ — Your teacher when you were a junior high school first year student was Ms. Tanaka, right?

③ うちらんとこは、めっちゃ都会じゃなかってんけど。 — Our place was not really in the big city.

④ うちんとこな、男十四人で
女の子一人やで。

My place (=my class) is fourteen boys and one girl!

⑤ 北海道も家ん中おったら暑くてTシャツで過ごしてるらしいよ。

I heard that in Hokkaido, if you are in the house, then it's warm enough to get by with only a T shirt on.

⑥ なんか水ん中にどれだけおれるとか競争したりした。

I did things like compete to see how long I could stay under water.

⑦ 山口ん家に忘れた。

I forgot it at Yamaguchi's house.

⑧ 大学ん時におばちゃん家に住んどった。

I lived with my aunt when I was a university student. (Note that the double ん in おばんちゃんんち reduces to a single ん.)

11-3 こん, そん, あん, どん

Similar to the particle の being pronounced as ん, the の sound in the definite particles この, その, あの and どの can be pronounced as ん in VJ. Thus, the VJ forms are こん, そん, あん and どん respectively. As is the case with the reduction of the particle の to ん, speakers tend to only use the reduced definite particle forms in very-frequently occurring morpheme bundles. Again, as with particle の, even then, the actual usage of reduced forms is still very rare. Similar to the genitive marker, over 90% of the examples found in the *Corpus of Kansai Vernacular Japanese* occur before one of four words. In this case the four words are 時, 中, だけ, and ぐらい. Here are some examples of the use of the reduced forms of the definite particles before these three words.

| VJ | こん・そん・あん・どん+時・中・だけ・ぐらい | ●○○ |
| SJ | この・その・あの・どの+時・中・だけ・ぐらい | |

EXAMPLE SENTENCES:

① そん時{とき}印象{いんしょう}とかどんなんやったんですか？ — What was your impression like at that time?

② あたしあん時{とき}やばかった。 — At that time, I was horrible.

③ こん中{なか}で使{つか}うのたぶん二{に}、三個{さんこ}しかないですね。 — Among these, there are probably only about two or three of them that I use.

④ もう生{い}きて行{い}かれへん、もうそん中{なか}で倒{たお}れてしまうねやんか。 — It is just that you cannot go on being alive, you will collapse in there (due to the heat).

⑤ なんかその時{とき}はちっちゃくて、こんぐらいやった。 — Well, at that time, it (the monkey) was quite small, about this big.

⑥ 演劇部{えんげきぶ}の思{おも}い出{で}ってそんぐらい？ — Is that all of your memories from drama club?

⑦ そんだけで十分{じゅうぶん}やわ。 — That much is enough.

⑧ 俺{おれ}どんだけ頑張{がんば}ってると思{おも}ってん？ — Just how hard you think that I'm trying?

⑨ うちもそんぐらいやったな。 — I also did about that much.

⑩ どんぐらい要{い}るんかな？お金{かね}。 — How much do you need? Money, that is.

11-4 Nominalizer ん

In the Japanese language, a verbal phrase can be changed into a nominal phrase by adding こと on to the end of it. This is called the gerund form. Gerund forms follow the same grammatical patterns as nouns, and therefore they can be used as the subject of a sentence or the object of a verb.

In conversational Japanese, の tends to be used as an alternative to こと. English uses the verbal suffix *-ing* to accomplish the same thing. Compare the following examples. The verbal phrases that have been changed into nominal phrases are highlighted.

◇ He swims every day.
◇ His swimming has improved.
◇ 彼は毎日泳ぐ。
◇ 彼は泳ぐのが上手になった。

In VJ, の can optionally be realized as ん. This has a very strong vernacular feeling to it, and it is a rather rare pattern. Nevertheless, it does occur, and being able to use this pattern will help your comprehension of VJ.

|VJ| VP ん
|SJ| VP こと, VP の

EXAMPLE SENTENCES:

① 俺意外と声高いの気にしてたから、人前でこんな声で歌うんは嫌やなと思った。
I'm really sensitive that my voice is exceptionally high-pitched, so I don't like singing in front of people with this voice.

② 風呂洗うんは、その日最後に入った人や。
Washing the bathtub is done by the person who had a bath last on that day.

③ 毎日、二時間半ぐらい行くんが、ちょうどベストや。 | Going every day for about two and a half hours is the best.

④ A. どんな夢見るの？ | A. What kind of dreams do you have?
　B. あの、よく見るんは悪夢が多いんや。 | B. Umm, of the ones that I often see, nightmares are common.

⑤ 若い人にはしんどいんやからな、正座ゆうんはあんまりないな。 | Well, it's really tough for young people, so sitting *seiza*-style is rare.

⑥ 辞書調べるんはめんどくさいな。 | Looking it up in a dictionary sure is a pain.

11-5 こんなん, そんなん, あんなん, どんなん

Vernacular Kansai Japanese contains a set of commonly-occurring phrases based on the SJ expression こんなの. The SJ consists of こんな plus the nominalizer の. The word こんな means 'this sort of.' The nominalizer の is added onto the end to form an NP. Thus, こんなの means 'this sort of thing.' This expression may refer to any concrete or abstract noun that the speaker has in mind.

As mentioned in the previous section, the nominalizer の may be pronounced as ん in VJ. Thus, the phrase こんなの may be pronounced as こんなん.

The Japanese language has several groups of phrases based on the こ そ あ ど series, such as the group この, その, あの, どの, and the group こう, そう, ああ, どう. The phrase こんなん also belongs to such a set. In this case the set is こんなん, そんなん, あんなん, どんなん. Following are some examples of these words used as nouns.

VJ	こんなん, そんなん, あんなん, どんなん •••
SJ	こんなの, そんなの, あんなの, どんなの

EXAMPLE SENTENCES:

① 自分のお母ちゃんが料理下手やから、もうこんなん食べてたらあかん。

My mother is bad at cooking, so I thought I really shouldn't have to be eating this sort of thing.

② 嬉しいやんか、こんなんができるわって思って。

I was happy, and I thought, "Wow! I can do this sort of thing."

③ 知らん、そんなん。

I have no idea about that sort of thing.

④ 余裕やで、そんなん。

That sort of thing I can do with room to spare!

⑤ テレビドラマであんなんあるけど。

There is that sort of thing in Japanese television dramas.

⑥ あんなん、なかなかないな。

It is rare that you find such a thing as that.

⑦ どんなん書くんやろ？

Hmm, what sort of thing will I write (for the calligraphy contest)?

⑧ 小さい企業ってどんなんなん？

What sort of place is a small company?

11-6 もん

The の sound in the word もの 'thing' can be realized as ん. Table 11-1 lists several SJ lexical items that contain the word もの, and their VJ counterparts.

SJ	VJ	English
物	もん	thing
食べ物	たべもん	food
飲み物	のみもん	drink
果物	くだもん	fruit
入れ物	いれもん	container
建物	たてもん	building
買い物	かいもん	shopping
織物	おりもん	fabric
変わり者	かわりもん	oddball

Table 11-1. Common vocabulary based on the word もん.

Here are some examples of the use of もん in VJ.

| VJ | もん |
| SJ | もの |

EXAMPLE SENTENCES:

① テレビはね、まあ観たいもんは一杯ある。 — As for television, there are lots of things (=shows) that I want to watch.

② 欲しいもんはもうないけど。 — There is nothing that I want.

③ 大体のもんはあったのよ。 They had pretty much everything.

④ 関西弁って言うもんは「なんでやねん？」とか。 That which is called Kansai dialect is expressions such as "Nande ya nen?"

⑤ 昔のダイエー行ってな、色々買いもんしてな、あっこにな。 In the past, I went to the Daiei department store, and bought lots of stuff there.

⑥ イタリアなんかおいしい食べもんがいっぱいありそうで。 It seems like there are many delicious things to eat in Italy.

11-7 Verbs ending in る before a nasal sound

Throughout the languages of the world, rhotic sounds tend to be weak. A rhotic sound is an r-like sound, such as the English sound 'r' and the consonant at the beginning of the sound ら. A weak sound is a sound that is sometimes omitted or changes to a different sound, depending on the dialect or the sound's location in a word or sentence. For example, 'r' tends to be omitted at the end of words in many varieties of English, such as British English. Another example comes from English loanwords in Japanese. When Japanese borrows a word from English that contains an 'r' near the end of a syllable, then the 'r' sound is ignored. This, the word 'card' has entered the Japanese langague as カード, without the 'r' sound.

The sounds る and ら are similarly weak in VJ, and in certain contexts may be realized as ん instead. This section and the next section introduces these changes.

In the case of る, this sound may change to ん at the end of a verb. For example, ある becomes あん, 食べる becomes 食べん, and 帰る becomes 帰ん. This variant form only occurs before a following nasal sound (な, に, ぬ, ね, の, and ん). This sound change is called assimilation. Assimilation sound changes result in two different sounds changing to be more like each other. In this case, the る sound changes to an ん sound in order to be more like the following nasal sound. Pronouncing two similar sounds in a row is easier than pronouncing two different sounds in a row, and therefore assimilation frequently occurs in spoken language.

| VJ | verb ending in る → ん before **n** | ••• |
| SJ | る (no change) | |

EXAMPLE SENTENCES:

① 何人か会った事あんねんけど。 — I have met a number of them.

② 会社で弁当注文できんねんやんか、毎日。 — Every day, I can order a *bento* lunchbox at work.

③ マネージャーっておんねんけど。 — There is a manager.

④ そこに小さいボールを投げんねん。 — You throw a small ball into there.

⑤ 名前を見たら時代が分かんねんな。 — If you look at someone's first name, then you can know how old they are, can't you?

⑥ 七年はかかんねんな。 — It will take seven years.

⑦ 辞書調べんの面倒くさいな。 — Looking it up in a dictionary sure is a pain.

In VJ, the SJ form verb て-form+ている reduces to verb て-form +てる. The る this form may further reduce to ん before a nasal sound.

| VJ | て-form+てる → てん before **n** | ••• |
| SJ | て-form+てる (no change) | |

136

EXAMPLE SENTENCES:

⑧ よく覚えてんな。 You remember it well.

⑨ あんたの両親さ、今二人と何してんの？ Your parents, what are the two of them doing these days?

⑩ 一応ＪＲが通ってんねんけど。 For what it's worth, the JR rail line passes through the town.

⑪ 駅からも離れてんねん。 It is far from the train station.

⑫ お母さんは、もうなんか怒んのが趣味みたいになってるから、怖い。 It is scary; it seems that getting angry has become my mother's hobby.

As introduced earlier in this chapter, the SJ particle の may be realized as ん. As this is a nasal sound, it is also the environment for the sound pattern る changes to ん. However, this results in a sequence of two ん in a row. In this situation, the combination ん+ん reduces to a single ん. Thus, 〜る+の may be realized as just 〜ん.

〜る+の → 〜る+ん → 〜ん+ん → 〜ん

As expected, this change has a very strong vernacular feeling to it. It is, however, fairly common.

| VJ | 〜る+の → 〜ん | ••• |
| SJ | 〜る+の (no change) | |

EXAMPLE SENTENCES:

⑬ どうすん？ What will you do?

⑭ あんた痩せてんちゃうん？ You lost weight, didn't you?

⑮ 今作りよんや。 I'm making it right now.

⑯ びっくりしとんは、人が多すぎる。 What was surprising was that there were too many people.

11-8 ない-form +んない

Another sound pattern involving ん occurs with Group I verbs that end in る, such as 分かる and 座る. In SJ grammar, the verb ending る changes to ら before the verbal negative suffix ない. Thus, the negative of 分かる is 分からない. In VJ, the ら sound may be realized as ん. In this case, the negative form of 分かる becomes 分かんない.

VJ	ない-form+んない
SJ	ない-form+らない

● ○ ○

EXAMPLE SENTENCES:

① 全然分かんないんすけど。 Well, it's just that I don't know at all.

② 今の髪型とあんまり変わんないね。 It was not so different from the hair style I have now.

③ 人の迷惑になってるのに、怒んないじゃないですか？ It is just that even though the kids are disturbing people, their parents don't get angry, isn't it?

④ 喋り出したら止まんないよね。 Once I start chatting, I can't stop.

⑤ 今は楽器全然触んないな。 These days, I don't touch musical instruments at all.

12 Abbreviation, Reduction and Omission

This chapter introduces several patterns involving the shortening of forms. As introduced in Section 1-1 (p. 9), forms sometimes shorten in vernacular language. This tends to happen more with grammatical words, but some commonly used lexical items also show shortening.

12-1 Commonly occurring abbreviations

This section lists several commonly occurring abbreviations. Each of these forms is a shortened pronunciation of either a common word, or a commonly occurring pair of words.

In some cases, it may seem like a shortening pattern can be applied to other related words. For example, consider the set of words これ, それ, あれ, and どれ. Of these, the word それ may combine with the particle は, resulting in the form そら. However, the combinations これ+は, あれ+は, and どれ+は do not shorten to こら, あら, and どら. The reason why only それ+は reduces to そら is because it is a morpheme bundle, as explained in Section 2-4 (p. 25). In other words, the definite particle それ and the topic marker は occur frequently together. In fact, the ratio of the frequency of occurrence in the *Corpus of Kansai Vernacular Japanese* of これは, それは, あれは, including the reduced form そら, is 21:184:34. That is, それは is almost eight times more frequent than either of the other forms. It is for this reason that only それ+は reduces.

Table 12-1 lists several abbreviated forms that occur with enough frequency to be worth learning. For each abbreviated form, the source of the abbreviated form and the corresponding SJ polite form are also given. Each expression is also rated for frequency and regional flavor.

Abbreviation	Source	Translation	Rating
いっか	いい+か	Is it good=enough?	●○○
えっか	いい+か	Is it good=enough?	●○○
そっか	そう+か	Is that right?	●●●
こっち	こちら	this way / one	●●●
そっち	そちら	that way / one	●●●
あっち	あちら	that way / one	●●●
どっち	どちら	which way / one	●●●
こんだけ	これ+だけ	just this (much)	●○○
そんだけ	それ+だけ	just that (much)	●○○
あんだけ	あれ+だけ	just that (much)	●○○
どんだけ	どれ+だけ	how much	●○○
あっこ	あそこ	over there	●●○
どっか	どこか	somewhere	●●●
こないだ	この+あいだ	these days	●●●
やっぱ	やっぱり	as expected	●●●
あんま	あまり	not so much	●●●
そら	それ+は	that + は	●●○
っちゅう	って+いう	see Chapter 9	●●○
つう	って+いう	see Chapter 9	●○○
いっちゃん	一番(いちばん)	most / best	●○○
見(み)して	見(み)せて	show	●○○
おかん	お母(かあ)さん	mother	●○○
おとん	お父(とう)さん	father	●○○
おっさん	おじさん	uncle / older man	●●●
しょ	しよう	let's do	●●○
しょん	し+よる+の	see Section 7-6	●○○
ちゃん	ちゃう+の	see Section 3-4	●●○

Table 12-1. A list of commonly occurring abbreviated forms.

12-2 [s] sound reduces to an [h] sound

Historically, an [s] sound in grammatical words such as それ and そう was changed to [h] in the Kansai region. For example, それ and そう became ほれ and ほう. The variant forms that start with [h] are now obsolete, having been replaced by their SJ counterparts, except for the two commonly occurring forms. This section is included more for those interested in the etymology of these two forms.

The first of these is the verbal negative suffix 〜へん (see Section 6-1, p. 62). This form is derived from the Old Japanese verb す. This verb is the precursor to the modern day verb する. Like its modern day variant, the Old Japanese verb す used an irregular inflection pattern. The verb inflected to せ before a negative or volitional suffix. The せ form is still seen in some modern day forms that have a very formal, archaic feel to them, such as せず and せよ. The Old Japanese verbal negative suffix was ぬ. Thus, the negative form of す was せぬ. In the Kansai region, the [s] reduced to [h], and the final [う] sound dropped off. These changes resulted in the modern day verbal negative suffix 〜へん.

せぬ → せん → へん

The second form which shows this change is the auxiliary verb はる, introduced in Section 5-5 (p. 59). This verb is derived from the verb 為さる, the honorific form of the verb する. The verb 為さる uses an irregular inflection pattern, and its 〜ます form is なさいます. Over time, なさいます reduced to なさい, and this form is seen in the pattern for commands, as in 食べなさい. In the Kansai region, 為さるchanged in different ways. The [s] reduced to [h] and the initial な sound dropped, resulting in the auxiliary verb はる. The grammar of はる is covered in Section 7.7, p. 84.

One more form that is sometimes mentioned in textbooks and heard in historical television dramas is the honorific suffix 〜はん. This form is derived from the SJ form 〜さん, which follows

141

a person's name, and also appears in the words such as お父さん and お母さん. These days, the 〜はん variant is only used by elderly speakers and comedians who are intentionally trying to speak with a heavy Kansai dialect.

12-3 Conjunctions

As introduced in Section 2-2 (p. 20), conjunctions play an important role in VJ. Conjunctions are also often commonly occurring set of expressions made up of smaller parts. For example, the conjunction それで is formed from the pronoun それ and the particle で. These two parts occur frequently together, and therefore they are a morpheme bundle (see Section 2-4, p. 25). Because they are a morpheme bundle, they are prone to reduction. Furthermore, many of the conjunctive forms are based on the words それ and そう. Both of these words start with an [s] sound. As introduced in the previous section of this chapter, historically [s] was optionally pronounced as [h] in grammatical words. Many of the conjunctive forms based on それ and そう use the ほれ and ほう variant forms. Table 12-2 lists VJ conjunctions and the SJ forms that they are based on.

Of these, which are worth remembering and using? Unless you have a particular interest in traditional Kansai dialect, you only need to be able to understand and use five of the VJ expressions: ほんで, で, んで, ほんなら and それじゃ. These are highlighted in gray. The first three, ほんで, んで, and で, all mean 'and then.' The other two both mean 'in that case.'

12 Abbreviation, Reduction and Omission

VJ	Source
ほたら	そしたら
ほいたら	そしたら
そえで	それで
そいで	それで
そんで	それで
ほれで	それで
ほんで	それで
ほいで	それで
ほいて	そして
で	それで
んで	それで
へて	そして
そえから	それから
ほんなら	それなら
んなら	それなら
ほんなん	それなら
ほんな	それなら
ほいから	それから
それじゃ	それでは

Table 12-2. A list of VJ conjunctions. The most common expressions are highlighted.

12-4 Case marker omission

One characteristic of VJ is that the case markers を, に, は, and が may be omitted. However, the rate of omission depends on the case marker. The direct object marker を shows the highest rate

143

of omission, and in fact it is omitted roughly 85% of the time in the *Corpus of Kansai Vernacular Japanese*. The other three case markers are deleted about 60% of the time.

Note that for all four of these case markers, the rate of omission is over 50%. This high rate of omission means that in VJ, including a case marker is the exception. If you include too many case markers in your speech, you will sound like a textbook.

Several linguistic factors influence the rate of omission. In general, case markers are omitted more often from simple sentences. (The idea of simple versus complex grammar was introduced in Section 2-1, p. 19.) In order to understand better case marker omission, first consider their grammatical role. Case markers clarify the relationship between a noun and a verb, such as subject of the verb, or direct object of the verb. If the relationship between a noun and an object is obvious, then the particle is not necessary. (Recall that speakers often omit unnecessary words and morphemes in vernacular language.) The most obvious relationship is that between a direct object and a verb, when the verb immediately follows the direct object. Compare the following two sentences:

◇ ご飯を食べる 'eat dinner'
◇ ご飯をレストランで食べる' 'eat dinner at a restaurant

The first sentence is simple, and the direct object occurs directly in front of the verb. The relationship between ご飯 and 食べる is obvious. The case marker を is often omitted from such sentences. In comparison, the second sentence is not as simple. The direct object does not occur directly in front of the verb, and therefore the relationship between ご飯 and 食べる is less obvious. The case marker を is omitted relatively less often from such sentences.

Another factor is the directness of the relationship. The relationship between direct objects, which is indicated by を, is more obvious than the relationship between indirect objects, which is indicated by に. Compare お金あげる with 先生あげる. The meaning of the first example is clear: 'give money.' The second example, on the other hand, is not so clear. It might mean 'give to teacher' or it might mean 'give teacher to someone else.' Since omitting を is less confusing, を tends to be omitted more frequently than other particles.

The final factor is noun complexity. A complex noun phrase consisting of a noun and a relative clause is more complex than just a simple noun. Consider the following two sentences:

◇ ご飯を食べる   'eat dinner'
◇ お姉さんが作ってくれたご飯を食べる   'eat the meal that my sister made'

The object of the verb in the first sentence is simple. In contrast, the object of the verb in the second sentence, which is modified by a relative clause, is more complex. Therefore the を in the first sentence tends to be omitted more frequently than the を in the second sentence.

From a linguistics perspective, case marker omission is a fascinating phenomenon, as it gives us insight into how the brain works. However, the influence of these factors is subtle and you need not concern yourself with such details while actually speaking Japanese. Rather, you should take a more intuitive approach: If it feels right, then omit the case marker.

Following are several example sentences illustrating case marker omission. In order to make it obvious where the omission took place, the omitted case markers have been replaced by empty boxes.

EXAMPLE SENTENCES:

① 平日の日□、何□してるの？   What are you doing on weekdays?

② あれ□飲もうか、これ□飲もうかと思うんやけど。   Well, it's just that I'm thinking should I take this (medicine) or should I take that (medicine).

③ 炭酸□飲んで、アイスクリーム□食べて、ホットケーキでも食べようみたいな。 I'm, like, let's drink pop, eat ice cream and eat pancakes!

④ 服□脱いで、お風呂□入ったんかな。 I guess that he got undressed and took a bath.

⑤ そこ□行ったら、全然ちゃうかった。 I went there but it was totally different.

⑥ 鍵□開けれんかった。 I couldn't unlock the door.

⑦ 警察の人□おんねんやんか。 There is a police officer there.

⑧ 新婚旅行□北海道□行ってんやん。 We went to Hokkaido for our honeymoon.

12-5 Copula omission

Another characteristic of VJ is that the copula may be omitted. Naturally, this only happens when the copula is in the non-negative non-past form や. In the case of a question, the following question marker (normally の in conversational Japanese) is also omitted.

Following are some examples of copula omission. As in the previous section, the location of the omission is indicated by an empty box.

VJ	copula omitted
SJ	〜です, 〜ですか

EXAMPLE SENTENCES:

① 出会いは大学□。 Our first meeting each other was in university.

② 施設の職員が三人□。 The facility's staff is three people.

③ 旦那さんが神戸の人□。 Her husband is from Kobe.

④ バンクーバー、田舎□？　　Is Vancouver in the countryside?

⑤ もらえるのは廃棄だけ□？　So you can only receive (and take home with you) the ones that are thrown away?

⑥ 朝はパートの人ばっかり□？　Is the morning staff part-time workers only?

⑦ 年齢によって違うわけ□。　The reason is that it's different for each age.

⑧ そう□、そう□。　　Yeah, yeah, that's right.

12-6 Shortening of long vowels

In VJ, the long vowels of certain forms may be pronounced as short vowels. However, not every long vowel may be shortened in this way: Only the long vowels of grammatical morphemes may be shortened. Thus, for example, 高校 'high school'—a lexical word— may not be pronounced as ここ. (Although there are some exceptions, which will be introduced in Chapter 13.)

So only vowels that express grammatical meaning may be shortened. What does this mean? Consider the form 食べよう 'let's eat.' The 食べ part of the form contains the lexical meaning: It indicates which verb. This is the verb's stem. The よう part contains the grammatical meaning: It indicates the intention of the speaker. This is the verb's suffix. The long vowel in よう is an example of a component with only grammatical meaning, and it is also an example of a long vowel that may reduce to a short vowel.

Often the boundary between the lexical part and the grammatical part is not so clear. For example, the volitional form of the verb 行く 'go' is 行こう. In this form, the lexical part, いこ and the grammatical part, こう, seem to overlap. Nevertheless, this overlap does not block the reduction of the long vowel, and 行こう may be shortened to 行こ.

This section introduces some examples of a long お reducing to a short お. The next chapter of the book introduces some grammatical patterns that result in long vowels other than just お. The long vowels resulting from those patterns may also be reduced to short vowels.

The long お seen in the volitional form of the verb and copula (polite SJ: 〜ましょう, でしょう) is often shortened. The following are some examples of the shortening of the long お in volitional forms.

| VJ | volitional form (short sound), やろ, でしょ | ••• |
| SJ | ます-form+ましょう, でしょう | |

EXAMPLE SENTENCES:

① 私も、もうこれ買おか、あれ買おか、と思うんやけども、止めた。 — I'm also thinking of buying this and buying that, but I decided not to.

② 知ってる、知ってる。見に行こ。 — Oh yeah, I know that. I should go see it.

③ 後で食べよ、後で食べよと思った。 — I thought, "Let's eat it later. Let's eat it later."

④ でもこれどうしよ、どうしよって思っとった。 — But I thought, "Oh man, what should I do about this?"

⑤ 変な子やろ。 — She's a strange child, isn't she?

⑥ 好きな映画、何やろなー。 — Hmm, what movie do I like?

⑦ 死にはせんでしょ。 — Well, it's not like you are going to die.

⑧ ラッキーって感じでしょね。 — You were lucky, weren't you?

The shortening of a long お sound also occurs in the grammatical words そう and どう, as seen in the examples ⑨ through ⑫.

12 Abbreviation, Reduction and Omission

|VJ| そ, ど
|SJ| そう, どう

EXAMPLE SENTENCES:

⑨ そやんな、やっぱ。 Yeah, that's right, as expected.
⑩ あ、そや、間違えた。 Oh, that's right! I was mistaken.
⑪ 昔はどやったん？ What was it like in the past?
⑫ うーん、どやろ。分からん。 No... what was it? I don't know.

    Several other examples of long お shortening are introduced in Chapter 14. Besides those examples, there are also a limited set of other words and in which the long お sound may be pronounced as a short お. Table 12-3 lists these words. These are lexical words, therefore they violate the rule that only the long vowels of grammatical morphemes may be reduced to short vowels. However, they are not nouns, and such exceptions are very rare. Finally, all of these expressions are frequently occurring expressions, and as explained frequency tends to lead to reduction.

VJ	SJ
めんどくさい	面倒くさい
かっこいい	格好いい
ほんとに	本当に
おはよ	おはよう
ども	どうも
ありがと	ありがとう

Table 12-3. A list of words in which a long お is often pronounced as a short お.

12-7 Abbreviations of proper nouns

Abbreviations occur frequently in the speech of youth. Many of these abbreviations are temporary slang that disappear from usage after their novelty has faded. However, some words stay. These words become a part of everyone's lexicon, not just the language of youth. Abbreviations for proper nouns in particular tend to be used by everyone. Everyone knows the abbreviated names for the local parks, schools, and restaurants. This section introduces such abbreviations.

When new abbreviations are formed, they tend to be of a certain length. Length is measured in a unit called the mora. Short vowels and the sound ん are one mora. The small っ used to indicate a geminate sound (a doubled consonant), such as in the word 学校 'school,' is also one mora. Long vowels are two moras. Thus, the word 学校 is four moras long, while 日本 is three moras long.

Shorter expressions are always preferred over longer expressions. However, if an abbreviation is too short, it loses the ability to uniquely identify the proper noun with which it is associated. The ideal length seems to be three mora. However, there is one more important factor. Many proper nouns are written in kanji. Abbreviations never truncate kanji readings. For example, the kanji 学 is read as がく. An abbreviation that uses this kanji will always keep the reading as がく, and never reduce it to just が.

Abbreviations of words written in kanji tend to take the first kanji from two of the morphemes in the name. Therefore, since there are many more two mora kanji than one mora kanji, abbreviations based on kanji tend to be four moras long.

In contrast, abbreviations of katakana names do not necessarily have restrictions. Therefore, katakana names can be reduced down to three moras.

Table 12-4 lists some commonly occurring abbreviations of proper nouns that you may encounter while talking in Japanese. Note that almost every abbreviation of kanji proper nouns is four

12 Abbreviation, Reduction and Omission

Full word	Abbreviations	English
University names		
東京大学	東大	Tokyo University
京都大学	京大	Kyoto University
大阪大学	阪大	Osaka University
神戸大学	神大	Kobe University
関西学院大学	関学	Kwansei Gakuin Uni.
関西大学	関大	Kansai University
同志社大学	同大, 同志社	Doshisha University
立命館大学	立大, 立命	Ritsumeikan Uni.
Transportation		
阪急電鉄	阪急	Hankyu Railway
神戸電鉄	神鉄	Kobe Railway
京阪電鉄	京阪	Keihan Railway
関西国際空港	関空	Kansai International Airport
Restaurants		
マクドナルド	マクド	McDonald's
ケンタッキー・フライド・チキン	ケンタ	Kentucky Fried Chicken
鳥貴族	トリキ	Torikizoku
餃子の王将	オーショー	Gyoza no Ohsho
CoCo壱番屋	ココイチ	Coco Ichibanya
ミスタードーナツ	ミスド	Mr. Donuts
スターバックス	スタバ	Starbucks

Table 12-4. Abbreviations for some commonly occurring proper nouns.

moras long, whereas those of katakana proper nouns are often three moras long.

If you are studying at a university, then ask some of the local students to teach you some abbreviations. You will find that almost every proper noun, such has the names of buildings, faculties, departments, and courses, have abbreviated names.

13 Patterns Seen in Adjectives and Verbs

13-1 Consonant doubling

In VJ, speakers often add emphasis to an い-adjective by slightly changing the pronunciation. The most common change is a doubling of a consonant at the beginning of the second syllable. Table 13-1 gives several examples of this. This pattern can be applied to any い-adjective that contains a consonant at the beginning of the second syllable. Note that the VJ forms for the words 大きい and 小さい use pronunciation patterns that are unique to those two words. This pattern is common, and does not have such a strong vernacular feel to it. This pattern is used throughout Japan. Table 13-1 lists some examples.

VJ	Source	Meaning
あっつい	熱い	hot
たっかい	高い	tall, expensive
やっばい	やばい	dangerous, awesome
きっつい	きつい	tough, tight
でっかい	でかい	big
くっさい	臭い	stinky
おっそい	遅い	slow
すっくない	少ない	few
むっずかしい	難しい	difficult
きったない	汚い	dirty
おっそろしい	恐ろしい	scary
おっきい	大きい	large
ちっさい	小さい	small
ちっちゃい	小さい	small

Table 13-1. Examples of consonant doubling in い-adjectives.

Consonant doubling does not occur with **w** and **y**. Two example words with these sounds are 可愛い 'cute' and 強い 'strong.' In these words, ん is inserted after the first syllable instead of consonant doubling. Table 13-2 gives some examples.

VJ	Source	Meaning
つんよい	強い	strong
かんわいい	可愛い	cute
こんわい	怖い	scary
よんわい	弱い	weak

Table 13-2. Examples of ん insertion in い-adjectives with **w** and **y**.

Some adjectives are also abbreviated at the same time. Table 13-3 gives some examples. In contrast to the above list, these words have a stronger vernacular feeling associated with them due to the inclusion of an abbreviated component.

VJ	Source	Meaning
あったかい	暖かい	warm
うっさい	うるさい	noisy, irritating
むっずい	難しい	difficult
きんもい	気持ち悪い	disgusting
おんもろい	面白い	interesting
めんどい	面倒くさい	bothersome

Table 13-3. Examples of consonant doubling / ん insertion and abbreviation in い-adjectives.

13-2 Clipping

Another way that speakers add emphasis to an い-adjective is by clipping the end of the adjective so that the word-final い is not pronounced. For example, 高い 'expensive' is pronounced as たか. Furthermore, this pattern may combine with consonant doubling. In this case, 高い is pronounced as たっか. The following are some examples of clipping. These forms are somewhat common, and have a somewhat strong vernacular feel to them.

EXAMPLE SENTENCES (THE CLIPPED WORDS ARE HIGHLIGHTED):

① 十万もすんの？ たっか。　　It costs 100,000 yen? Expensive!
② あ〜、だる、みたいな感じ。　It was like, ahhh, I'm feeling so lazy today (だるい = feel lazy).
③ かるっ！　　　　　　　　　So light!
④ ダンス部見て、すごって思って。　I saw the dance team and thought, "Awesome!"
⑤ A. 二十歳で嫁に来たんやで。　A. I came as a bride when I was 20 years old.
　 B. はっや。　　　　　　　　B. So soon (=young)!

13-3 Vowel coalescence

This section introduces vowel coalescence. The word 'coalescence' means to merge together to create something new. There is a variant form of い-adjectives in VJ in which the final い vowel is merged with the preceding vowel to create a new sound. However, coalescence only occurs if the preceding vowel is either **a**, **u**, or **o**, and does not occur with a preceding **i** or **e** sound. Why not? In the case of **i**, an **i** sound followed by い does not result in a change of pronunciation. As for **e**, there are no い-adjectives in the Japanese language that end in **e**+い.

The combined vowels result in a single, long vowel. The resulting long vowel depends on which two vowels are merged, as shown in Table 13-4.

Vowel Combination	Result	Example
a+い	**e**+え	高い→たけえ
i+い	no change	可愛い
u+い	**i**+い	熱い→あちい
e+い	Does not occur.	
o+い	**e**+え	遅い→おせえ

Table 13-4. Vowel coalescence in the base form of adjectives.

Vowel coalescence combines with both consonant doubling and clipping. Thus, the い-adjective 高い may be pronounced as たかい, たか, たっかい, たっか, たけえ, たけ, たっけえ, or たっけ. As has been repeated several times throughout this book, one of the characteristics of vernacular language is multiple ways of saying the same word.

Vowel coalescence does not combine with ん insertion (see Table 13-2). The resulting form is too far removed from the SJ form.

The following are some examples of vowel coalescence. Note

that these forms are rather rare, and have a very strong vernacular feel to them. For each variant form, the original い-adjective form is also given in brackets.

[VJ] すげえ (vowel coalescence) ●●○
[SJ] すごい

EXAMPLE SENTENCES (THE ORIGINAL FORMS ARE IN BRACKETS):

① すげえ【すごい】、この人って。 — Wow, this guy is really something.

② いって【痛い】！ — Ouch!

③ 校長先生の話なげえ【長い】なって思ったのは、すげえ【すごい】覚えてる。 — I really remember that the principal's speeches were always so long.

④ 彼怒ってさ、「うるせえ【うるさい】んだよ」って怒鳴った。 — He got angry and yelled, "Shut up!"

There is one exception to the above pattern that needs to be pointed out: The い-adjective いい 'good' may be optionally pronounced as ええ. This is very common form, and it does not have as strong of a vernacular feeling to it as the above forms. Following are some example sentences containing the ええ variant.

[VJ] ええ ●●●
[SJ] いい

EXAMPLE SENTENCES:

⑤ お風呂入ったら気持ちええよな。 — Taking a bath feels wonderful, doesn't it?

⑥ もうええかって思う。 — I felt that it was enough.

⑦ あんたええ勉強しよってる
やろ、私の話聞いて。

Listening to my stories, you are really learning a lot, aren't you?

⑧ スタッフさん、めっちゃ仲ええねんな。

The staff get along really well, don't they?

13-4 k-dropping

The adverbial form of an い-adjective is formed by dropping the word-final い and adding く. Thus, the adverb of 速い 'quick' is 速く 'quickly.' Historically, the k sound was omitted in the Kansai dialect of Japanese. Thus, the Kansai dialect adverbial form of an い-adjective was formed by dropping the word-final い and adding う. Furthermore, the う sound merged with the preceding vowel to form a single, long vowel. This is another type of vowel coalescence, but this time with the う vowel. The resulting long sound is listed in Table 13-5. Note that the **i+**う results in a small ゅ that combines with the sound before it.

Vowel Combination	Result	Example
a+う	o+お	はやく→はよお
i+う	ゅう	美味しく→おいしゅう
u+う	**u+**う	悪く→わるう
e+う	This combination does not occur.	
o+う	o+お	よく→よお

Table 13-5. Vowel coalescence in adverbial form of adjectives.

As these forms involve a vowel change, they have a very strong vernacular feeling. (Forms that change the pronunciation of SJ have a strong vernacular aspect to them.) Generally speaking, these forms are obsolete with some very important exceptions. First, these forms are still used by elderly speakers. Second, younger speakers and comedians use these forms when they are making an effort to speak the Kansai dialect with a strong flavor. Third, two forms—よお and はよお—are used with such a high frequency that they have become morpheme bundles (as described in Section 2-4, p. 25). The first form, よお, is based on the い-adjective 良い, and it is the VJ variant of よく. The second form, はよお, is based on the い-adjective 速い / 早い, and it is the VJ variant of はやく. These two forms are used frequently by speakers of all ages, and they are worth knowing. Below are several example sentences containing よお and はよお.

However, before presenting the example sentences, it first needs to be pointed out that since the form はよお contains a long vowel in the grammatical part, you can optionally apply the pattern of a long vowel reducing to a short one, as introduced in Section 12-6 (p. 147). (Note that はよお is another example in which the lexical and grammatical parts seem to overlap, as explained in Section 12-6.) Thus, はよ is another variant form of the SJ form はやく. Interestingly, よお also contains a long お sound but it seems that it does not shorten to just よ. In spite of there being over 700 examples of よお used as a variant form of よく in the *Corpus of Kansai Vernacular Japanese*, there is not a single example of the shortened form よ.

| VJ | はよ(お), よお (common k-dropping) | ●●○ |
| SJ | はやく, よく | |

EXAMPLE SENTENCES (THE ADVERBIAL IS HIGHLIGHTED):

① メールは、よおせんから。 I don't do email much at all.
② ずいぶんとよおなってます。 It has become much better.
③ 結構、仲よお遊んだ。 I played together quite well.
④ あの時自分は、よお麻雀やっとった。 At that time, I sure did play mahjong a lot.

159

⑤ うそ？もっとはよ教えてや。 — No way! Tell me these things sooner!

⑥ はよお仕事が済んだら、それでええねん。 — If you finish work early, well that is fine.

⑦ はよ出てけ、はよ卒業しろ、って言われとった。 — I was told you better move out soon, you better graduate soon.

⑧ 次の日の朝、はよおから仕事。 — The next day, I have work from early on.

The following are some examples of k-dropping in forms other than よお and はよお. Again, note that these forms are now really only used by elderly speakers, and they are included here for the sake of completeness. Remember that the resulting long vowel is often shortened. The following example sentences contain examples of both shortened and unshortened vowels.

| VJ | 悪う, 強お (rare k-dropping) | ●○○ |
| SJ | 悪く, 強く | |

EXAMPLE SENTENCES (THE ADVERBIAL IS HIGHLIGHTED):

⑨ 昔の言葉使う人は少のなったな。 — People who use the language of the past have become quite few.

⑩ 少のうなったよ。昔はもっとあったから。 — They've become few. There were more in the past.

⑪ それはな、悪うは言えへん。 — As for that, well, I cannot say anything bad.

⑫ 戦争がひどなって向こうの状態が悪なったから。 — The war had become quite terrible, and the situation over there had become quite bad.

⑬ ほいでまた、はよう来たり
おそう来たりする人とか。

And then, also, some people came early and some people came late.

⑭ きつう言われた。

I was spoken to in a harsh manner.

⑮ それが、あのー、しんどなってたわ。

That was, well, it had become quite tiresome.

⑯ 血圧は高なったし。

His blood pressure has become high.

　　The 〜く suffix occurs in two other い-adjective forms besides the adverbial form. The first form is with the suffix 〜て as 〜くて, as in the example 小さくて速い 'small and fast.' This is the conjunctive form. The second place where 〜く occurs is before the negative suffix 〜ない, as in the form 大きくない 'not big.' Both of these forms were historically environments for k-dropping. However, similar to the adverbial form, the variants without the k sound are now limited to the speech of the oldest speakers. Even the forms base on the adjectives 良い and 速い / 早い, such as the forms よおない and はよおない, are very rare.

　　Generally speaking, you should not use these forms in daily conversation unless you are making a specific effort to speak with an exaggerated Kansai accent, although you may hear such forms if you speak with elderly people.

　　Several example sentences have been provided for the sake of completeness.

| VJ | 悪うて, 強おて (rare k-dropping) | ●○○ |
| SJ | 悪くて, 強くて | |

| VJ | 悪うない, 強おない (rare k-dropping) | ●○○ |
| SJ | 悪くない, 強くない | |

EXAMPLE SENTENCES (THE K-DROPPED FORM IS HIGHLIGHTED):

⑰ 片<small>かた</small>づけんのにもう、しんどおて。   Tidying up was also very tiresome.

⑱ やからもう熱<small>あ</small>うて熱<small>あ</small>うてな。   Because it was hot, so hot.

⑲ 日産<small>にっさん</small>やで。悪<small>わ</small>うないよ。   It was a Nissan. They are not a bad car, you know.

⑳ 成績<small>せいせき</small>だけで見<small>み</small>れば全然<small>ぜんぜん</small>よおない。   If you just consider my grades, then they were not good at all.

㉑ なんかパソコンそんな強<small>つよ</small>おないで。   Well, I'm not so good at using a personal computer.

In section 1-1, it was pointed that the further away a vernacular form is from the standard form, the more vernacular it feels. Look again at Table 13-2. Among all of the changes listed in Table 13-2, the change **a+う→o+お** results in the greatest deviation from the standard pronunciation, since not only is the k dropped, but the vowel sound also changes. It seems that such a large change is too much for many speakers. These speakers use an alternative form in which the ～く is dropped, but the preceding vowel quality is not changed. thus, for example, 高<small>たか</small>くない 'not tall / expensive' becomes たかない. This option is an alternative to **a+う→o+お** that does not sound as extreme. The following are some examples.

[VJ] 悪<small>わる</small>, 強<small>つよ</small> (alternative k-dropping)	●●○
[SJ] 悪<small>わる</small>く, 強<small>つよ</small>く	

EXAMPLE SENTENCES (THE K-DROPPED FORM IS HIGHLIGHTED):

㉒ 食<small>た</small>べ物<small>もの</small>はそんな高<small>たか</small>なかったんちゃうんかな。   Food wasn't that expensive, I don't think.

㉓ え？五時半<small>ごじはん</small>に起<small>お</small>きた？早<small>はや</small>ない？   Huh? You got up at 5:30? Isn't that early?

㉔ やれる時間が少ななるってのを考えてなかった。 I didn't feel that the time that I could do it had become short.

13-5 Small っ changes to う

The て-form +て and て-form +た of Group I verbs that end in う, つ, or る contains a small っ. For example, the て-form of 会う, 立つ, and 帰る are 会って, 立って, and 帰って respectively. The small っ represents a doubling of the following consonant. In VJ, in some specific cases the small っ may be pronounced as う. The specific cases that allow for the alternative pronunciation are a preceding **a**, **u**, or **o** sound. Thus, 会って and 立って may be pronounced as あうて and たうて, but 帰って cannot be pronounced as かえうて.

Furthermore, the う vowel coalesces with the preceding vowel as shown in Table 13-6. This table should look familiar to you, as the patterns are similar to those presented in Table 13-5.

Vowel Combination	Result	Example
a+う	**o**+お	買って→かうて→こおて
u+う	**u**+う	言って→ゆうて
o+う	**o**+お	取って→とうて→とおて

Table 13-6. Vowel coalescence in the て form of verbs.

These changes are heard throughout western Japan, and they have a very strong vernacular feeling to them. Finally, note that the resulting long sound is in the grammatical part of the word. As explained in Section 12-6, the long sound in the grammatical part of the word may optionally be shortened. The following are some example sentences illustrating the use of these changes. In some cases, the long sound has been shortened.

| VJ | て-form+うて, て-form+うた |
| SJ | て-form+って, て-form+った |

●○○

EXAMPLE SENTENCES:

① タバコ吸うてもいい？ May I smoke?
② 北海道もええかなーとか思おた。 I think Hokkaido might be good too.
③ で、これ自分で買おたん？ And so did you buy this by yourself?
④ この時計合おてるん？五分ぐらいは進んでるんちゃうん？ Is this clock correct? Isn't it five minutes fast?
⑤ お金も毎日使てたし。 I were using some money every day.
⑥ 空襲に遭おて死んだ人もあるわけや。 For that reason, there were people who died in air raids.

It needs to be pointed out that the change of the small っ into う is very common with the verb 言う. Even if you personally do not use these forms, you need to understand the alternative forms for this verb, and you should even consider using this form yourself when speaking Japanese in a casual context: The vernacular variants for 言う using う in the place of っ are simply that common. Once again, note that long sound may optionally reduce to a short sound.

| VJ | 言うて, 言うた |
| SJ | 言って, 言った |

●●●

EXAMPLE SENTENCES:

⑦ あんた何を言うてんねん What in the world are you saying?
⑧ みな友達同士で行こうか、言うて。 And they were saying, "How about all of us friends go together?"

⑨ 全部言たらあかんやん、それ。　You must not tell all of it!

⑩ 簡単に言うたら、「愛」。　Simply put, it's love.

⑪ そんなん言たら、うちの家やばいから。　If you put it that way, then our family is in trouble!

⑫ 「お金ないわ」とか言うとる人をどう思いますか？　What do you think of people who claim that they have no money?

13-6 Reduced forms of the verb しまう

SJ contains the verb しまう, which is mostly used after the て form of a main verb as an auxiliary verb. By adding the auxiliary verb しまう after a て form, the speaker implies that the action or outcome was unintentional, and that it may have had unforeseen or undesirable consequences, as in the example 忘れてしまった 'Oh no! I forgot!'

The verb しまう may also be used as the main verb. In this case, it is just an exclamation expressing regret towards an action that was unintentional or undesirable, as in the example しまった 'Oh no!'

This verb has several variant pronunciations in VJ. These pronunciations make use of several of the patterns introduced in this chapter and the previous chapter. The first of these is that small つ may be pronounced as う in the て and た forms of the verb. The う sound then combines with the preceding **a** sound, resulting in a long お. That is, しまって may be pronounced as しもおて in VJ. As with the other verb forms that involve a change in the vowel of the verb stem, this form has a strong vernacular feeling to it. The following are some example sentences.

VJ　しもおた　●○○
SJ　しまった

| VJ | て-form+てしもおて, て-form+てしもおた | ●○○ |
| SJ | て-form+てしまって, て-form+てしまった | |

EXAMPLE SENTENCES (THE ORIGINAL FORMS ARE IN BRACKETS):

① こんな昔の話、もう忘れてしもおて【忘れてしまって】ね、君。　This stories from such a long time ago, you have forgotten them, haven't you?

② もう半分以下に減ってしもおて【減ってしまって】、今、スキー人口が。　These days, the skiing population has decreased to less than half.

③ そこで病気になってしもおて【なってしまって】な、あの盲腸やな。　And then I got sick there, and it was appendicitis.

④ 恋愛してしもおたら【してしまったら】、そら、しゃあないけどなあ。　If you have fallen in love, then, well, there is nothing that can be done about that.

⑤ あの中途半端なことしてしもおた【してしまった】から今後悔しとる。　Now I'm regretting that I ended up doing such a half-baked job at that time.

The VJ form also shows a pattern similar to the clipping pattern introduced in Section 13-2 (p. 155). In this case, the front of the form is clipped. Thus, しまう becomes まう. Similarly, しもおて becomes もおて, and しもおた becomes もおた. Following are several examples illustrating the use of these clipped forms.

VJ	て-form+てまう, て-form+てもおて	●○○
SJ	て-form+しまう, て-form+しまって	●○○
VJ	て-form+てもおた	
SJ	て-form+てしまった	

13 Patterns Seen in Adjectives and Verbs

EXAMPLE SENTENCES (THE ORIGINAL FORMS ARE IN BRACKETS):

⑥ 全部好き、食べてまう【食べてしまう】ねん。 — I like them all, and I think I'll end up eating all of them.

⑦ やっぱ緊張してまう【してしまう】。 — As expected, I end up getting nervous.

⑧ 悪口になってまう【なってしまう】んやけどさ。 — It is going to end up sounding like I'm bad-mouthing them.

⑨ そんなん見つけてさ、笑ってまう【笑ってしまう】やん。 — If that is found out, then everyone will end up laughing at you.

⑩ もう母親はな、もうぼけてもおてん【ぼけてしまってる】ねん、もう全然。 — My mother has already gone senile, completely senile.

⑪ 単位落としてもおた【落としてしまった】。 — I ended up failing the course.

⑫ もう終わってもおた【終わってしまった】から。 — Unfortunately, it has already finished.

⑬ うわあ、切ってもおた【切ってしまった】、みたいな。 — And then he was like, "Oh no! I accidentally cut it!"

The forms with a long お sound also have a variant form with a short お. This is another example of the pattern that a long お sound reduces to a short sound (introduced in Section 12-6, p. 147).

| VJ | て-form+てもて, て-form+てもた | ●○○ |
| SJ | て-form+てしまって, て-form+てしまった | |

EXAMPLE SENTENCES (THE ORIGINAL FORMS ARE IN BRACKETS):

⑭ 電車ん中で寝てもて【寝てしまって】。 — I ended up falling asleep on the train.

⑮ それが癖なってもて【なってしまって】ね。 That has become a bad habit.

⑯ この前も飲み会で終電が終わってもて【終わってしまって】、タクシーで帰ってん。 This past drinking party, I missed the last train and ended up coming home by taxi.

⑰ 年寄りばっかりになってもて【なってしまって】な。 It has become so that there are just elderly people now.

⑱ お茶が冷めてもた【冷めてしまった】な。 Oh, your tea has become lukewarm.

⑲ 忘れてもた【忘れてしまった】、恥ずかしい。 I'm embarrassed, but I have forgotten.

13-7 Reduced forms of the verb もらう

There is one more verb that shows the patterns introduced in the previous section. That verb is もらう 'to receive.' This verb also shows the pattern of a small つ being pronounced as う in the ～て and ～た forms of the verb. Here also the う sound combines with the preceding **a** sound resulting in a long お sound. However, over time, the form もろおて further reduced to もおて. This is another example of Not this. Thus, the VJ forms for もらって and もらった are もおて and もおた. Unsurprisingly, these forms have a strong vernacular feeling to them. Following are some example sentences.

| VJ | もおて, もおた | ●○○ |
| SJ | もらって, もらった | |

| VJ | て-form+てもおて, て-form+てもおた | ●○○ |
| SJ | て-form+てもらって, て-form+てもらった | |

13 Patterns Seen in Adjectives and Verbs

EXAMPLE SENTENCES (THE ORIGINAL FORMS ARE IN BRACKETS):

① 当時三週間で十三万もおた【もらった】ん。

At that time, I got 130,000 yen for three weeks of work.

② そのもおた【もらった】お金で遊びに使たらえらいこっちゃ【ことや】で。

If I used the money that I received to go and play then I would be trouble (literally. it would be a huge thing).

③ 親から金もおたら【もらったら】、あとで、ぐずぐず言えんやろ？

If you received money from your parents, you can't really complain about that now, can you?

④ 京大の人に教えてもおてん【もらってる】の？

Were you taught by someone from Kyoto University?

⑤ 稲刈るのも、機械買おてもおて【買ってもらって】な、それで稲刈りしてん。

As for the rice harvest, I got (=had bought for us) a harvester, and I used that to harvest the rice.

⑥ その近所のお医者に診てもおた【診てもらった】。

I was examined by a local doctor in the neighborhood.

⑦ 紹介してもおた【してもらった】んが、じいちゃんや。

The one who was introduced was my grandfather.

⑧ 簡単に家族構成とか、教えてもおて【教えてもらって】いい？

Can I have you simply (=quickly) introduce your family make-up?

13-8 Reduced forms of ～て+いく

You are most likely familiar with omitting the い in ｜て-form｜+て+いる. Thus, 食べている 'eating' is normally pronounced as 食べてる in spoken Japanese. Similarly, the い in ｜て-form｜+て+いく is also optionally omitted. The pattern ｜て-form｜+て+いく means to go after performing some action, as in the example 食べていく 'eat and then go,' or to have some action gradually shift either physically or metaphorically away from you, as in the example 減っていく 'gradually decrease.' The reduced from いく tends to be either in the plain form or the ｜ない-form｜; the other inflections are not used without the initial い.

VJ	｜て-form｜+てく, ｜て-form｜+てかん	●○○
SJ	｜て-form｜+ていく, ｜て-form｜+ていかない	

EXAMPLE SENTENCES:

① ターンして戻ってく？ — Shall we turn around and go back?

② 出かけるときいつも持ってくねん。 — I always bring it with me when I go out.

③ どっか持ってかなあかんの？ — Do we need to bring this somewhere?

④ どんどん進んでかなあかん。 — We must gradually progress forward (away from this point).

⑤ 食べて寝るから余計太ってくで。 — If you eat and then go to sleep, you will gain a lot of weight.

13-9 ～て+や/あ～ Combine to Form ～た～

The last pattern to be introduced is the て-form て-form followed by the auxiliary verbs やる and あげる. The pattern て-form+あげる means to do some action to the benefit of someone else. The pattern て-form+やる has the same meaning as て-form+あげる, but it is only used when the benefactor is social inferior to you (for example, the pet dog or a young child). In both of these cases, the verbal suffix ～て combines with the following sound, either や or あ, to become た. For example, the verb 教える 'tell / teach' followed by やる and あげる becomes 教えたる and 教えたげる respectively. These combined forms follow the same verbal inflection paradigms as やる and あげる. These forms have a vernacular feeling to them, and the form て-form+あげる should not be used with someone who is superior to you.

| VJ | て-form+たる | ●○○ |
| SJ | て-form+やる | |

EXAMPLE SENTENCES (THE ORIGINAL FORMS ARE IN BRACKETS):

① 数学は無理やけど、それ以外やったら全部教えたる【教えてやる】。
Math is impossible, but I'll teach you anything other than that.

② こいつ殴ったろ【殴ってやろ】かな、って思ったけど。
I thought, "I want to give this guy a punch."

③ 君も奥さんもうたら、奥さん守ったらん【守ってやらん】とあかんで。
If you receive a wife (old-fashioned way of saying to get married), then you must protect your wife.

| VJ | て-form+たげる | ●○○ |
| SJ | て-form+てあげる | |

EXAMPLE SENTENCES:

④ 水なかったら水入れたげなあかん【入れてあげなければならない】。 — If there is no water, then put some water in.

⑤ まー、したげる【してあげる】人は少ないけど。 — Well, there are few people who will do that for you.

⑥ 一日も休まなかったら本を買ったげる【買ってあげる】わ。 — If you don't miss a single day (of school) then I'll buy you a book.

［著者略歴］

Kevin Heffernan（ケビン・ヘファナン）
関西学院大学総合政策学部教授

1970年カナダ生まれ。1991年に交換留学生として初来日。トロント大学にて博士号（言語学）を取得。2009年より現職。専門分野は日本語における言語変化や口語的バリエーションの研究。

著書：Kevin Heffernan（2013）"Introduction to Communication for Japanese Students" くろしお出版。

The Grammar of Kansai Vernacular Japanese

2019年2月28日初版第一刷発行

著　者	Kevin Heffernan
発行者	田村和彦
発行所	関西学院大学出版会
所在地	〒662-0891
	兵庫県西宮市上ケ原一番町1-155
電　話	0798-53-7002
印　刷	協和印刷株式会社

©2019 Kevin Heffernan
Printed in Japan by Kwansei Gakuin University Press
ISBN 978-4-86283-272-6
乱丁・落丁本はお取り替えいたします。
本書の全部または一部を無断で複写・複製することを禁じます。